The Book of *New* Family
TRADITIONS

How to Create Great Rituals for Holidays and Everyday

by Meg Cox

Illustrated by Sarah McMenemy

RUNNING PRESS
PHILADELPHIA · LONDON

For Dick, my partner in rituals and all else.

9   8   7   6   5   4   3

Digit on the right indicates the number of this printing

Library of Congress Cataloging-in-Publication Number 2002108929

ISBN 0-7624-1442-1

Cover and interior illustrations on pages 15, 21, 28, 32, 34, 38–39, 42, 46, 53, 55, 58, 62, 68, 73, 82, 84, 100, 110, 113, and 123 by Sarah McMenemy
Design and interior illustrations on pages 24, 37, 41, 47, 49, 50, 51, 57, 63, 69, 78, 88, 89, 96, 97, 103, 106, 108, 109, and 124 by Corinda Cook
Edited by Lynn Rosen
Back cover photograph © Chris Bierlein
Typography: Avenir and Baskerville

This book may be ordered by mail from the publisher. Please include $2.50 for postage and handling.
But try your bookstore first!

Running Press Book Publishers
125 South Twenty-second Street
Philadelphia, Pennsylvania 19103-4399

Visit us on the web!
www.runningpress.com

Contents

Introduction:
Celebrate Your Family

Family traditions are wonderful, and it is a special joy to celebrate a holiday or carry on a bedtime ritual just as our parents and grandparents did. But the fact is, our lives are very different, and we need to invent new traditions for today's families. Let's face it, our grandmothers didn't need a tradition for dropping off the kids at daycare or dealing with stepfamilies at holidays.

When I became a mother in 1994, I started a personal quest to find great contemporary family rituals that would inspire and instruct me. I wanted to find rituals that were simple but profound, practical and fun. Using my career skills as a journalist, I spent more than three years interviewing diverse families all over the country and compiling a collection of inventive new traditions, everything from "Family Happiness Parties" to "Overcoat Day," one family's quirky way of welcoming winter.

I wanted to find and share new rituals for birthdays and holidays, bedtime and dinnertime, but I also sought fresh ways of celebrating established holidays like Thanksgiving and July 4. Not to mention a whole compendium of unexpected traditions: sports rituals, pet rituals, homework rituals, vacation rituals and family meetings, among others.

I use both tradition and ritual to describe the special ways families celebrate, but I'm going to use the word ritual more, and here's why: the dictionary says that traditions are "beliefs and customs handed down from generation to generation," whereas a ritual is "an action repeated" or "an established procedure for a religious or other rite." I think ritual can convey something more recent and spontaneous: something we've done just twice and plan to do regularly. And something small and daily. Ritual is a much more inclusive word, covering the vast range of life's compelling ceremonies, from a simple grace or goodbye hug, to elaborate festivities like Christmas and weddings.

I like to say that family ritual is pretty much anything families do together deliberately, as long as it's juiced up with some flourish that lifts it above humdrum routine. Repeated words or actions, special food or music, or a heightened sense of attention can provide the juice. I wouldn't call it a ritual if you sometimes sit on the front steps and blow bubbles with your kids, but if you do it every Friday and then have graham crackers and milk and call it your "welcome-to-the-weekend party," that's definitely a family ritual.

Most of my favorite rituals are extremely simple, like the woman who writes inspiring messages in colored chalk on her driveway and street for her daughters to find on the first day of school. Or the father who provides "monster spray" in a spritzer bottle, so his son can fall asleep every night feeling protected.

Ritual is a package deal. It's everything we do to celebrate our families, not just on special occasions but also every day, every meal, every bath and every bedtime story. In ritual, little is big: although dress-up holidays with lavish feasts are fun, it's the everyday traditions that determine how we experience our families, and demonstrate hands-on love to our children.

Intuitively, we know this is good, and consciously pass down beloved traditions from our own childhoods. But the power of ritual and the need for it are far stronger than we realize.

Anthropologists have never found a human culture without ritual, and psychologists say it's the early comfort rituals we perform with our infants that give them the sense of security essential for human growth. Knowing there is always someone there to pick you up and kiss the boo-boos makes it possible to keep taking steps into the vast unknown.

Even the most bewildered new mom quickly realizes that her baby gets calmer with a settled routine for sleeping, eating, and other activities. And if you start singing a funny little song every time you get ready to dip her in the baby tub, she starts cooing in anticipation: the two of you are in a private sorority, and she loves knowing the secret handshake. Through rituals and traditions as simple as this, you are building the bond of your joined identity, defining your relationship by acting it out.

Ten Good Things Rituals Do for Children

Impart a Sense of Identity

Provide Comfort and Security

Help to Navigate Change

Teach Values

Pass on Ethnic or Religious Heritage

Teach Practical Skills

Solve Problems

Keep Alive a Sense of Departed Family Members

Help Heal from Loss or Trauma

Generate Wonderful Memories

There's no question that creating and sustaining family traditions takes effort. But if you enter into ritual-making with an understanding of its awesome, multiple benefits, you will never want to stop.

Comfort and security are two of the most important benefits of early ritual, and these are not just things we need as babies. I know a family that used to have a "poor sweet baby" blanket, and any time a family member had a setback at school or work, the rest of the family would take the blanket out of a closet and wrap it around the suffering one. Even the father, an Episcopal priest, would be thus comforted on a bad day, with his wife and children hugging him in the blanket, and chanting in unison, "Poor sweet baby!"

Rituals also provide a sense of identity: Religious families build their beliefs into every tradition from high holidays to bedtime prayers. Sports-crazed families often have sports-related rituals, while musical families sing together. Children grow up feeling Mexican or Chinese partly because of ethnic celebrations and ritual foods. Kids who grow up feeling close to their extended families are those who regularly attend family reunions, or go to "cousins camp" at Grandma's every summer.

Next to rituals of celebration, which include

birthdays and holidays, the biggest category is probably rituals that help children handle transitions. Bedtime rituals, for one, are all about helping infants and children switch gears from activity and togetherness to stillness and solitude.

But there is so much more going on. Rituals need to be conscious because they also pass on our values. That's why many families add rituals of philanthropy to their holiday festivities, and don't just focus on gift-giving. And rituals can be designed to teach practical skills, like families where the kids take turns making Sunday dinner (even if they start off serving peanut butter sandwiches).

Savvy parents realize early that one of the most practical uses of ritual is in problem-solving. Do the kids bicker constantly? Create a tension-diffusion ritual. Having a crisis every time you drop your toddler off at daycare? Design a good-bye ritual that helps her feel loved but independent, ready to explore new ground.

Ritual is also an important tool in helping families heal in times of stress or loss, whether it's the backyard funeral for a beloved pet or the loss of the Little League championship. Looking back on the aftermath of the 9/11 terrorism, there was a constant focus not just on the loss, but also on the rituals of mourning and healing, from New York Fire Department bagpipes to the planting of a million daffodils around New York City. Victims' families handled grief with their own private rituals, like the little boy who ran around in his backyard every night waving a burning sparkler up to his dad in heaven.

Ellen Galinsky, co-founder of the Families and Work Institute and the author of such books as *Ask the Children*, has done ground-breaking research on what kids really think of their lives and their parents. When she asked kids what they would remember most from their childhoods, Ms. Galinsky learned that it wasn't big gifts or fancy celebrations, but simple rituals and everyday traditions: modest but personal gestures of love, like made-up bedtime stories, that left the children feeling safe and cherished.

Knowing that these daily acts form the core of what our children will carry through life, we need to choose our traditions carefully. Instead of a struggle over bedtime each night, how much better that our children still remember the special back rubs we gave them, and the stories that we told.

The special power of ritual is that it can slow time and heighten our senses, and by doing so, we can intensify and deepen our family ties. Learning simple ways to create unforgettable traditions is what this book is all about.

Ritual Recipes:
Getting Started

The mission of this book is to give parents the tools and encouragement to fill their family lives with memorable, meaningful traditions. But when and where do families *need* rituals and traditions? And how do they create them?

Many families start with holidays, a natural place to begin. There are also the rituals that just creep up on us; you serve pancakes with chocolate chips one Sunday, and the next Sunday, the kids wonder, "Why aren't we having the special Sunday pancakes?" A ritual is born.

But where else do rituals belong? What is enough? Can there be too many? What is the recipe for ritual?

There is no minimum daily requirement of ritual prescribed by the USDA or child psychologists, but if I had to reduce ritual life to a formula, I'd give families three goals to meet.

First, research and experience suggest that families should have one solid ritual of connection daily, and I recommend they also plan a modest weekly family ritual. In addition, all major milestones, accomplishments, and relevant holidays deserve to be celebrated, leaving enormous leeway to individual families about which occasions they mark, and how. Thirdly, I suggest applying rituals as a corrective whenever there's a bumpy spot in the regular routine. Transitions are always tough for young children; substituting a fun or silly ritual for a ritual of tantrums and fussing can miraculously smooth over rough patches.

Daily rituals of connection don't have to take up much time, and can take many forms. The important thing is that every family member gets to act or speak. Some families have breakfast together and compare their thoughts about the day ahead. Some perform a group hug or family cheer. Other families find it easier to connect after school each day, or at dinner or bedtime.

The Kyger family in Free Union, Virginia, saves its connection ritual for dinner. After a simple Quaker grace, during which family members briefly hold hands and pray silently, each person around the table has to share a "new and good" about their day, even the teenagers. Another family has a bedtime ritual called "gratefuls and grumbles," where the children have to come up with one of each, but end with the positive note of something for which they are grateful.

Suzy Kellett, a divorced mother of quadruplets, had "teatime" with her kids, now grown, every evening around 9 p.m. The kids would stop doing homework, hang up the phone, and gather in the family room for 20 or 30 minutes. In addition to imbibing cinnamon herbal tea, the Kelletts were drinking in each other's moods and stories. All of us change continually, and such "check-in circles" allow us to witness one another's transformations, while also celebrating what stays constant in our connection.

Weekly rituals also vary widely, including weekly meetings or a designated "family night." One family has a weekly "pizza night" at home, but they structure the meal to include family business. They may tell jokes and rate their favorite sports teams while eating pizza, but over dessert, they always discuss current family issues, anything from behavior concerns to vacation ideas. It's also fine if the weekly get-together is "movie night" in your family room. But in that case, it's even more important to build in a conversational give-and-take component. Saying "please pass the popcorn" doesn't qualify as a ritual of connection.

Many religious families use a weekly family night to help pass on their faith, devoting part of the evening to prayer. Some families have a meeting format, maybe half an hour that includes a review of everyone's schedule that week and a discussion of chores. To make it fun, this is also a good time to pay the kids their allowances or designate a family "winner of the week" based on attitude and accomplishments, and end with a special snack.

In the following pages, this book will offer detailed ideas for holidays and celebrations, but families should also be on the lookout for unconventional milestones. Maybe your child isn't ever going to be an Olympic swimmer, but finally conquered a longstanding fear of getting his face wet or completed his first real dive. To celebrate such spontaneous triumphs, keep a package of instant brownie mix in your pantry. Make a brownie sundae, or use a star-shaped cookie cutter on the brownies to properly celebrate his stardom.

One of the most rewarding but under appreciated uses of ritual is to smooth over rough spots in a family's regular routine. Take the mother who had trouble getting her kids out of bed after weekends—she invented "Monday sundaes" for breakfast (frozen yogurt, fresh fruit, and sprinkles), which only get served to kids who are dressed and downstairs inside her time limit.

Ingredients:
The Three Parts of Ritual

But once you know you want a ritual, how do you make one?

There is no "Joy of Rituals" cookbook, but after interviewing hundreds of families across the country and trying lots of rituals with my own family, I've developed some basic "recipes" for making memorable traditions.

A satisfying and thorough ritual has three parts: it has a beginning, a middle, and an end. Even a simple grace before supper has those elements: a nod or ver-

bal cue that grace is to be said, the grace itself, and "amen" at the end. These are similar to the three stages anthropologists observe in tribal rites of passage: first comes preparation, then action (and often transformation, say from boyhood to manhood), and finally the stage of integration and celebration.

The reason you need some sort of beginning is that ritual is human life in capital letters: it needs to be punctuated, capitalized, elevated. Ritual requires intense focus, and a good ritual beginning gets the participants engaged. It tells people a ritual is starting, like the rising curtain before a theater performance.

A common way to signal a ritual's start is by sound: a verbal cue, or special music, or tapping a fork against the side of a glass. Visual cues work too.

If you think about a simple birthday celebration, the "beginning" is as basic as turning out the lights before presenting the cake. The "action" stage is when the child blows out candles and makes a wish while everybody sings "Happy Birthday." In the final or celebration stage, cake is eaten and gifts opened.

Ritual beginnings make us aware that something special is about to happen, functioning like the "Once upon a time" of a fairy tale. But in order for the narrative of ritual to keep us absorbed, there must be something compelling to pull us along. These are a creative combination of dramatic elements: ritual words and actions, often accompanied by ritual food and ritual music. But special doesn't have to mean complicated. Your ritual food can be lemonade and Goldfish® crackers, and your music as simple as a child's drum or a bedtime lullaby.

Anatomy of a Ritual

My family's winter solstice celebration is an example of a simple but meaningful ritual that combines special actions, music, and food.

Step 1: After dark, turn out all the lights and sit in darkness, remaining silent for at least a full minute. Then, talk about how darkness makes you feel, and how joyful primitive people must have been knowing that the days would soon lengthen. Next, light candles and run to the front door, flinging it open as you yell, "Come back, sun!"

Step 2: Combine orange juice and vanilla ice cream in the blender to make "sun shakes."

Step 3: Play the Beatles song "Here Comes the Sun" while drinking the shakes, and discuss all the good things that come from the sun.

A simple ritual doesn't have to include music plus food plus action plus words. It might have just one or two of those elements, but it becomes cherished through repetition, like families who develop elaborate hugs or handshakes for bedtime or good-byes.

In the Bonner family of Baltimore, Maryland, the kids make up wacky names for bedtime hugs, most of which their mother must invent on the spot. "Give me a squirrel hug," they'll say, and after she interprets that request, they'll want a cuddly "kitten hug" followed by a "rocket hug," where she whooshes them skyward. Although the hugs vary every night, the ritual has been a bedtime staple for years.

The Two P's:
Find Your Purpose and Make It Personal

The seed for a ritual's form grows directly from its purpose. That includes everything from holidays to problem-solving rituals. Figure out your purpose; then you can imagine creative ways to achieve it that suit your family.

Take this problem-solving ritual: After they were in a minor car accident, the Sutton family vowed they would never again forget to buckle their seatbelts, so they decided to invent a seatbelt ritual. The purpose, of course, was buckling, which became the ritual "action," but this had to be preceded by a simple beginning to cue the behavior, which turns out to be Mary Sutton, the mother, saying, "Buckle up, everyone!" After they buckle, Mary asks her three kids why they do this, and they all chorus back, "Because we love each other!" This qualifies as a "celebration" ending: the kids may not get cake or cookies, but there is an emotional payoff.

The first year my son went trick-or-treating, I invented the Good Witch of Halloween. My purpose was this: I was afraid he'd want to eat that huge candy hoard and I wanted to find a fun reason for it to disappear. Since Max's birthday was two weeks later, I told him to put his plastic pumpkin of candy outside his bedroom door the night before he turned three (until then, he's only allowed one piece a day). The Good Witch of Halloween would come and take the candy for poor children and replace it with a small birthday gift, which he would find when he awoke. Not surprisingly, my son loves this ritual, and it achieves my goal.

For a Thanksgiving ritual, the purpose is to give thanks. But when it comes to narrowing down the millions of possible ways to do that ritual-wise, it's helpful to focus on another P—make it Personal. Take something from your family's history or passions to create a ritual of thankfulness that will be much more meaningful than a generic ritual because it is specific to you.

One family I know that loves to camp dresses up like Pilgrims and Indians each Thanksgiving, and canoes out to an island where they put on a rather primitive outdoor feast (they precook the turkey). Another family of avid needleworkers started a special tablecloth ritual for Thanksgiving: every person at the table signs their name in pen on the cloth, and the family matriarch later embroiders over the signatures, a different color each year. Then there's the family whose ancestors nearly starved out west, surviving one bad year only on turnips; they include a turnip dish every Thanksgiving, thankful they have so much else to eat now.

Ritual Actions

The bigger and more ceremonial the occasion, the more elaborate the ritual, and the more attention must be devoted to the ritual's central action. But what is the right action for a ritual? One that powerfully expresses the core emotional truth of the ceremony.

Think of the actions within a wedding, and the way in which the ceremony combines speaking with doing. It isn't just the vows that make us feel married, but also the action of placing rings on each other's fingers. The circle is a powerful symbol of eternity, and we are placing this physical object around a part of another person's body. A designer wedding dress, elegant flowers, and a string quartet will add to the atmosphere, but this simple act is the emotional core of the ritual.

But sometimes, there is no ritual pattern to follow. I decided, for example, to invent a ritual when I changed my name to that of my husband. To me, this seemed to require a sort of baptism. I decided I needed to submerge myself and asked my friend if I could dive into her swimming pool before witnesses—in a dress. I spoke to the group before I dived, and afterwards, we celebrated with cake and champagne. I changed into a new t-shirt, on which was painted my new name.

I've thought a lot about what constitutes a major milestone in a child's life, and how those can be marked. One way, borrowed from tribal rites of passage, is to create a threshold, an actual barrier that the child must cross through as he or she acts out this important transition. There are lots of ways this can be done, including having them break through tissue paper that's been taped across a doorway. I know a private preschool where the kids "graduate" by walking across a bridge made of wooden blocks; they are literally embraced by the kindergartners waiting on the other side. You could also organize a "love gauntlet," two parallel rows of people, and gently push the celebrated one down the line.

In the case of my son, I've created thresholds using painted sheets, which are taped to the entrance over the family room. I cut a slit up from the floor, and he has to cross through the sheet to get to his presents. (See birthday section for details.)

Simple actions become profound when placed in a context of ritual focus and meaning: when I wanted to create a womanhood ritual for my niece on her 13th birthday, it was mostly about the words I spoke, but they carried extra weight because we were standing inside a circle of sparklers on the beach, in the dark.

If a ritual is about letting go, then the action of burying something in the ground is a possibility, or releasing helium balloons. We did the latter after scattering my father's ashes on the golf course. Tied to each balloon was a farewell message to my dad, and seeing those bright balloons swept out of sight by the wind evoked a visceral feeling of release.

If you can't think of a ritual action, a great place to start is by mentally going through the list of four elements (earth, air, fire, and water), and asking if any of them fit the core emotional truth. A ritual of remembrance, for example, could include lighting a candle (fire) and talking about a deceased pet or person, or planting a tree for them (earth).

Just remember this: Start with your ritual's purpose and let that guide you to a central ritual action. Your best chance of success is to keep it simple, and be playful. If you set a tone of having fun, of everybody having their say, then family members won't feel awkward or too embarrassed to participate.

When starting a new ritual, it's vital to announce your plans in advance, so everybody knows what's coming. Kids love routine, so the first time you try a new ritual, they might be wary, and adjustments may be needed before the family embraces this new tradition wholeheartedly. (And family rituals often need tweaking over the years, giving kids a bigger role as they age.)

As I said earlier, bracket your central ritual action with a beginning and an end. It could be as simple as a declaration that "it's time," or perhaps turning the lights off for a second, or lighting a candle. Possible endings include a simple hug, a short prayer, or treat food you all share.

Don't worry about finding good ideas for new traditions. There are hundreds of them in the pages that follow. You can adopt these rituals and celebrations just as they are, or use them as the germ of a new idea. Even if the resulting ritual doesn't turn out exactly as you hoped, you will have captured time and created memories as a family, together.

Holidays

New Year's Celebrations

New Year's Family Blast

A great way to celebrate the coming of the New Year is to pay tribute to the year ending, while also welcoming the new year. Have a family-focused party and choose things from the following menu of ritual activities depending on how much time you have, and what suits you. Add your favorite food, drinks, music, and decorations.

Depending on your preference and the ages of your kids, you can do this on New Year's Eve or New Year's Day. If your kids want to ring in the new year but can't stay up till midnight, turn the clocks ahead.

Make Resolutions

Cut small strips of paper half an inch wide and about 6 inches long. Take whole walnuts and, using nutcrackers, carefully open the nuts and remove the nutmeat inside. Each person makes three resolutions and writes each one on a paper strip, which is then carefully folded and put into the nut. Glue each nut closed. Using markers, each person writes their name on a nut.

This idea comes from the Hilton family of Henderson, Nevada, who glue ribbons into their walnuts and use them to decorate their Christmas tree. They reuse the same nuts every year, and once they started the practice, they began a tradition of reading last year's resolutions aloud before writing new ones. That way they can review how well they've done. Nanette Hilton, the mother of four daughters, says she thinks it's great for her girls to see that "life is fluid. They see Mommy and Daddy working on goals too . . . and sometimes failing."

Tip: Also start a New Year's Resolution notebook in which everyone writes his or her resolutions down. Keep this book handy in a family room or kitchen drawer, so people don't forget their goals as the year goes by!

Review the Past Year

Sitting at the kitchen table or the family room sofa, look together at all the family photos you took in the past year, and/or watch the family videos. Then, everybody gets a chance to vote on the best and worst day of the past year. Also, everybody fills out this list:

> My most embarrassing moment this year was when I _____.
>
> I should have had my photo on the cover of *People* magazine because I _____.
>
> You guys can be annoying, but you really came through for me when _____.

Give annual family awards for "best athlete," "worst school picture." Use your imagination for more awards.

Toast the New Year

Use plastic wine or champagne glasses but serve sparkling water or cider to the kids. Each person gets to make a toast, saying one thing they hope happens in the new year to himself or herself, the family, or the wider world. End with a shared family toast "To the (Name) Family!"

Celebrate with a Burst

It's an ancient tradition to open the doors (and sometimes windows) to let the New Year and good luck into your home. It's also a tradition to make lots of noise, so get wooden spoons and bang on pots, pound drums, and ring any bells you have.

In Texas, the Minich family loves to make noise by bursting balloons, but the balloons are also full of "treasure," a good omen for a prosperous year ahead. Beforehand, the parents purchase about 500 balloons and fill them with a piece of candy or a coin, with a few containing dollar bills. The balloons are inflated with an inexpensive, handheld pump, then stuffed into a room that has mostly been emptied of furniture. At midnight, the family and their friends dive in and pop the balloons.

January 18: Celebrate the Birthday of A.A. Milne, *Winnie-the-Pooh* Author

Getting a sense that there is a person who creates the books and characters we love is a great way to make reading special and personal. Kids love knowing that A.A. Milne wrote the books about his real-life son, Christopher Robin, and his stuffed animals. In addition, mid-January is a good time for a party, deep in the winter doldrums.

Setup

Spread a picnic blanket or bedsheet on the floor of the family room or playroom. If there are any stuffed animals in the household from the Hundred Acre Wood (Pooh, Piglet, Tigger, Eeyore, etc.), place them on the blanket, along with paper plates or plastic ones from a child's tea set.

Foods

Since Pooh loves honey, serve honey graham crackers or honey cookies. If blowing out candles is important, use a cupcake. Drinks could be juice or herbal tea with honey.

Activities

Sing "Happy Birthday" to A.A. Milne, then blow out any candles and eat treat foods. Read some of Milne's work, either the classic books *Winnie-the-Pooh* and *The House at Pooh Corner* or his poems "When We Were Very Young" and "Now We Are Six." There are also some terrific, practical Pooh books from Disney, such as *Oh Bother, Someone's Messy*. If someone wrote a book about the stuffed animals in your house, what adventures would they have? Imagine the titles.

Some other favorite authors and their birthdays:

March 2: Dr. Seuss

How about green eggs and ham for breakfast or dinner?

June 10: Maurice Sendak

Dress up like wild things!

We got the idea for Milne's birthday from Kids Celebrate!: Activities for Special Days Throughout the Year by Maria Bonfanti Esche and Clare Bonfanti Braham.

Valentine's Day

What's Sweet About You Poster

This is like giving your kid a giant Valentine card, but much more personal. Make one for each child. If you're having a special dinner, you could bring the posters out then. Or prop them up against the kitchen chairs, so your kids find them when they come downstairs to breakfast or come home from school.

Materials

Large sheets of poster board in white, pink, or red (one sheet for each poster); red and pink construction paper; scissors; glue; small Valentine candies, such as chocolate hearts wrapped in foil; markers.

Instructions

Cut 9 to 12 hearts from the construction paper. The hearts should be about 4 inches high and 3 inches wide. On each heart, write one trait you love about that child's nature. Make it specific, focusing on positive aspects of their personality. Also, praise behavior you'd like to reinforce, such as putting away toys or progress in potty training.

Across the top of the poster, write "What's Sweet About (Child's Name)." Glue the hearts to the board, but just put glue on the bottom edges and up the sides of the hearts. Leave the top open, so they work like pockets. Put a piece of Valentine candy in each pocket.

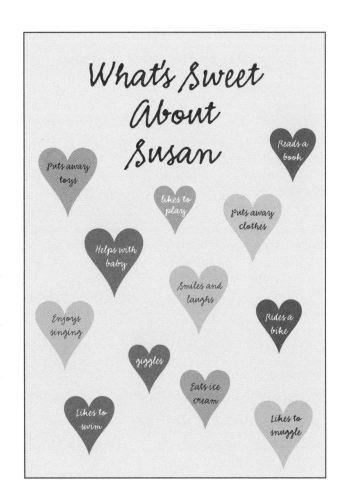

More fun ideas:

The Book of Love

Who wrote the Book of Love? You did. Buy an inexpensive blank book with a heart on the cover, or glue one there. Call it "The Book of (your last name) Love," and each year, have every member of the family write one loving thing about every other member (take dictation for young kids).

Red Food Night

At the Straw household in Plano, Texas, all the food for Valentine's dinner is red. Sue Straw serves beets or red cabbage, mashed potatoes mixed with red food coloring, and either ham (pink) or pasta with red sauce. Red fruit might include grapes, raspberries, or strawberries. Even the milk is red. Desert can be brown, as long as it's chocolate and shaped like a heart.

Valentine Tree

Trees are a great centerpiece of ritual action because they grow and change like families do, symbolize life and hope, and can be easily but beautifully decorated for any occasion. Every year, the Dodge family buys a small tree in a pot, and decorates it with a string of tiny white lights. They buy red craft paper and cut out teddy bears and hearts, poke holes in their tops, and use thin ribbon to tie them onto the tree. The decorations stay on until spring, when the family plants the tree in their yard. If you do this every year, you could designate a special Valentine Grove on your property.

Have-a-Heart Awards

Each member of the family gives an award to each other member for a special act of love or kindness. Buy round, fuzzy, ping-pong-ball-sized pom-poms at your local craft store, to which you can glue little eyes and mouths and feet. Cut hearts from a piece of construction paper 4 inches square, and glue the feet to the paper heart. Write on the heart the name of the person getting the award and what they did. Perhaps one child helped a younger sibling learn to tie his shoes. Perhaps Dad earned his award coaching Little League last summer.

Passover

The oldest holiday in Judaism, Passover celebrates the liberation of the Jewish people from slavery in Egypt some four thousand years ago. The observance lasts eight days but the highlight is the Seder, or formal family dinner, that begins the holiday. A Seder is guided by the Haggadah, a book that contains prayers, readings, songs, and stories, but there are thousands of published versions. Families freely create their own traditions for bringing the story vividly to life during the long meal. Here are highlights of some special family Seders:

Fleeing Egypt

At the appropriate moment during the Seder, the Brosbe family of Santa Rosa, California, has one of their guests ring the doorbell and run away, leaving a note on the front steps that says "GET OUT OF EGYPT NOW." The family and their guests strap on backpacks and rush out the back door, where they march around the backyard singing a traditional Passover song.

Emphasizing Freedom

Passover is a great time to talk about the joy as well as the responsibilities of freedom, then and now. Laurie Salen, a social worker in San Francisco, has everybody who comes to her Seder bring a symbol of their own liberation to put on the table. One brought termination papers from a hated job. A workaholic friend brought her dancing shoes, because she had finally fulfilled a fantasy of working less overtime and taking dance classes. A guest with AIDS brought some of the drugs that keep him free to enjoy life. At other Seders, people discuss countries in the world today where the citizens have limited freedom.

Acting Out the Plagues

Many families get creative in depicting the 10 plagues sent down by God when Pharaoh broke his repeated promises to free the Israelites. Some families take a blank roll of paper and tape it around the dining room like a mural, putting crayons on the table so the kids can draw each plague as it's described. Some discuss how modern-day plagues affect the world, such as AIDS.

Kid-Friendly Passover

Julie Stockler's Seders with her two daughters are especially playful. She has been known to use troll dolls to act out the story of the holiday (the troll with a star in his hand was God), and always has a "movie night" the week before so her girls can watch *The Ten Commandments* because "the plagues are so vivid." In trying to dress like ancient Hebrews, the family has wrapped themselves in bedsheets for the Seder, and once ate while lying down. While slaves, the Hebrews had not been allowed to recline while eating, a position reserved for free people, so some Seders are eaten while reclining.

An Intellectual Seder

When the Weber family of Los Angeles sends invitations to 30 or more people three weeks before the holiday, many of the guests are sent a question to discuss during the Seder. Sometimes an individual is asked to answer and sometimes a whole family. Often the guests do research to prepare their responses, and some families choose to put on a rehearsed skit. The end result is a stimulating discussion that lasts for hours, and just being asked is considered an honor. Some questions are repeated most years, but there is usually at least one new one. Some questions asked in the past are:

1. There is no mention of Moses in the Haggadah despite his importance to the story; prepare an argument to include Moses.

2. What are 10 plagues that threaten us today?

3. There are four questions traditionally asked at a Seder; develop four others to share with the group.

Some Passover Books and Websites

My Favorite Family Haggadah: A Fun, Interactive Passover Service for Children and Their Families, by Shari Faden Donahue, provides text and pictures for an abridged Seder that lasts just 20 or 30 minutes.

A Passover Haggadah, by Elie Wiesel, combines a full-length Seder text with historical and personal commentary by the Holocaust survivor and author.

www.aish.com/holidays/passover includes a history of the holiday from a Jerusalem-based educational organization, with family craft ideas such as a matzoh holder made of cardboard and fabric.

www.geocities.com/helenacan/Writings/Godly/Passover.html has extensive instructions for Christians who wish to hold a Passover Seder, including recipes.

Easter

Easter is the most important festival of the Christian church, and celebrates the resurrection of Jesus from the dead. The 40-day period leading up to Easter, called Lent, is generally a time of fasting, praying, and serious contemplation about suffering and the message God wanted to send with the death of Jesus. During Lent, devout Christians deprive themselves of things they especially enjoy, often foods like sweets or meat.

Washing Hands

Since Jesus washed the feet of his disciples, bring a bowl of water, soap, and a towel to the table one night at dinner, and have family members wash one another's hands, with care and tenderness. Talk about what it means to be a disciple, and the importance of being humble, even as a leader.

Handmade Crosses

Using simple twigs from your backyard and twine, have each member of the family fashion a simple cross. Each person can keep a cross on their bedside table, and hold it while praying and thinking about the suffering of Jesus on the cross.

Fasting Ritual

Fasting isn't a good idea for small children, but having occasional meals where the family eats less than usual is one way to ritually experience fasting. The next night, talk about whether everybody was a bit hungry when they went to bed, and what that felt like. One family tried an experiment of computing how much money a family their size would get for food for a week if they were on welfare; they spent only that much money at the supermarket, and ate only that food for the week.

Sunrise Bonfire

Light is a symbol of Jesus, and "seeing the light" figures in many hymns. At dawn, or as early as you can wake the family, walk outside and make or bring a light of some kind. You may choose to make a small "bonfire" in your yard (or even your outdoor grill), or have everyone bring a flashlight. Read from the book of Luke about the resurrection, and break your fast with sweet rolls or other treat food.

Most of these rituals were adapted from the Lenten Calendar provided by Alternatives for Simple Living, a nonprofit group dedicated to faith-based, nonmaterialistic celebrations. It includes activities and Bible readings for Lent, and can be found at **www.simpleliving.org**. Another good website is **www.marvelicious.com/easter.html**, where you'll find a history of the holiday, a recipe for hot cross buns, and such poems as "The Jelly Bean Prayer" ("Red is for the blood He gave, Green is for the grass He made . . .").

Easter Fun

Candle Ritual

Julie Young had just moved and needed a simple ritual. For the week leading up to Easter, she gathered some pretty candles and set them up in the living room. Right before bedtime, she would turn out the lights, light the candles, and read about "the events of Jesus' last week on earth" from a book called *The Book of God for Children*. Each child gets to blow out one candle before going up to bed.

Creative Egg Hunts

To avoid fighting over eggs, designate a color for each child and make sure there are the same number of each color hidden. Some people add extra eggs that are specially marked with an "X" or a sticker; anyone finding those eggs gets a special treat or prize. Betsy Muir's family in California has big family Easter celebrations with a double hunt: after all the plastic eggs are found the first time, they're rehidden in the house, often stashed somewhere on one of the grown-ups, such as in a pocket, shoe, or handbag. One family makes finding the Easter baskets more fun by hiding them in the house but attaching long ribbons to them; the kids wake up to find one end tied to the foot of their bed, then have to follow it to the basket.

Garden Celebration

Rain Mako in Arkansas celebrates Easter with her family as the earth's rebirth. They put a brightly colored flag at each of the compass points in the family garden, and the flag colors represent the four elements of earth (brown), air (blue), fire (red), and water (white). As they drive in the four stakes, they talk about how these elements are required by all living things. The family dresses up in party clothes, beats drums, and sings songs about spring. Many Christian churches have a tradition of Easter sunrise services, and dawn would also be a good time for a family garden ceremony.

First Day of Spring

The official beginning of spring, March 20 or 21, is marked by the vernal equinox, when the sun crosses the equator from south to north. Some fresh ways to mark this joyful transition:

Paint the Rocks

The landscape of winter is drab and bare, but colors will burst forth in the spring. One way to symbolize and celebrate that transformation is to color your surroundings. If it's not raining, grab some washable poster paints in primary colors and some big paintbrushes. Pour small amounts of paint into paper cups for portability, and go paint any rocks you've got on your property. Paint pictures of flowers, write words, splash and drip like Jackson Pollock. If you haven't got rocks, paint the driveway or use colored chalk. You might want to add favorite warm weather activities, like kite-flying or bubble-blowing, and mix up the season's first pitcher of lemonade.

First Picnic of the Year

The Suks of Evanston, Illinois, have a picnic on the first day of spring, no matter the weather. L'Tishia Suk prepares picnic food such as deviled eggs and iced tea and packs it in the family car along with a Frisbee, baseball, and bat. Their destination is the nearest park. Even if they have to eat in the car, trek through snow, and wear gloves, they throw out the first ball of the season.

Celebrate Big Bird's Birthday

Every year on the first day of spring, Big Bird celebrates his birthday, and he always turns six. If your kids love *Sesame Street*, you can adapt the idea of Susan Lynch of Merchantville, New Jersey, and mark this occasion at home. Her kids always make a cake with sprinkles on top to represent birdseed. They invite friends and hand out party favors like pinwheels or flowers. There are plenty of great *Sesame Street* and Muppet CDs, if you're looking for perfect singalong songs, though "Happy Birthday" is a must.

Plant Flowers

Kids love to dig in the dirt, and if the weather is bad, you simply plant in pots indoors. Best bet for small hands: nasturtium seeds, which are about the size of peas.

How to Make a Bird's Nest Basket

Birds flying north after the winter are looking for material to build their nests. You can help them and attract birds to your yard by supplying nest-making material in an inviting way.

Materials

Plastic berry baskets from the supermarket (use the ones your blueberries came in, or ask the produce department for some extras); short pieces of string or ribbon; feathers in muted colors (birds won't take anything in a bright color that might attract predators' attention); twigs and leaves.

Directions

Simply arrange the nest materials in the basket, then tie string or ribbon to the four corners and use string to hang the basket from a tree branch, preferably one you can see inside the house.

Arbor Day

National Arbor Day has been celebrated since 1872 and is observed in most states on the last Friday in April. Planting trees is a fabulous activity for families and a great opportunity to create hands-on environmental awareness. Trees produce oxygen, moderate the temperature, diminish smog, and provide a home for wildlife. Any kid can help dig a hole, stick in a sapling, and pour water on it.

You can always go to the nearest nursery and buy young trees, but if you're organized enough to plan ahead, an alternative is the National Arbor Day Foundation. For a $10 donation, the nonprofit group will mail you 10 young trees, a variety of types that will thrive in your part of the country. They will look like dead twigs when they arrive, only about a foot long, but they'll come with planting instructions and your kids can watch them grow, year by year. The toll-free number for the Arbor Day Foundation is 888-448-7337, and their website is **www.arborday.org**.

Tarrant Figlio has been celebrating Arbor Day with her kids for years, and they have developed some special rituals. "On Arbor Day, we always plant a tree together as a family. I tell the kids how special trees are and we talk about how birds nest and how paper is made from trees. They are sort of like mini-science lessons." Tarrant's children also keep a special scrapbook for their Arbor Day trees, and every year they measure each tree, count branches, and take a photograph. Since the picture includes the kids, they can look back and see how they grew, alongside their trees.

May Day

How to Make a May Day Basket

Materials

Paper plates, either floral or colored, or white ones if your kids would prefer to decorate and color them with crayons, markers, or stickers.

Instructions

Bend each plate into the shape of a cone, and staple the place where the sides meet. Glue or staple a pretty ribbon to the inside of the top of the cone, so you can hang the "basket" on someone's doorknob.

Fill the basket with daisies or other spring flowers, and if the recipient of the May Day basket won't be home, wrap the stems in a wet paper towel covered with plastic wrap to keep the plate dry.

Deliver the baskets to the homes of special friends and relatives.

In Casper, Wyoming, Mary Sutton's children often fill their May Day baskets with candy or homemade cookies instead of flowers. There are many elderly people living in their neighborhood, and they love to leave the baskets at their homes, anonymously. Her kids sneak up to the house, place the basket on the doorknob, ring the bell, and then run.

May Day Rituals

The first day of May is a fascinating holiday because its history is so diverse. Centuries ago in Europe, it was celebrated as a spring festival and fertility rite, with feasting, crowning of May Queens, and dancing around a maypole. Devout religious types frowned on all the wild drinking and partying, including the Puritans who came to this country. What celebration is done in the U.S. today tends to be somewhat muted, though flowers still figure as an important element, and some schools and community groups erect maypoles. In Hawaii, May Day is "Lei Day," and the local people drape one another with those colorful flower necklaces. Still another aspect is May Day's association with worker's rights: at the end of the 19th century, union organizers were fighting hard for the right to an eight-hour workday, and had big May Day rallies in support of this. Here are some ideas for families who want to mold this background into traditions of their own.

Flower Garlands

Flower crowns and garlands are lovely, but the flowers quickly die. Instead of using live flowers, get some small dried or silk flowers at a craft store, and using florist's wire and ribbon, make a crown to fit the head of each young girl in the family. Tie additional bright ribbons to the back, so they stream down past the girl's waist. Improvise your own May Day party and feast, with music and dancing. If you haven't yet, start working in your garden on this day.

Family Job Tree

To honor the history of labor in your family, create a family tree going back several generations that shows not only family members' names but also what work they did during their lives. Talk about the history of work and labor, the movement away from agrarian life in this country, and imagine jobs and work in future times, including the adulthood of your kids.

Flowers Forever

Kate Smith helps her kids gather flowers on May Day and then preserve them. They make a simple flower press, placing the blooms between two layers of cardboard, then squishing them together with heavy books such as phone books. Leave the flowers to dry and flatten overnight, then glue them to frames, turn plain paper into pretty stationery, or glue the flowers into a diary or other special book.

Mother's Day

Some Fun New Ideas

Breakfast Out of Bed

Judy Elkin finally confessed that she hated getting breakfast in bed on Mother's Day: all those crumbs in the sheets, plus she would rather eat with her kids than alone. So her family came up with a creative twist: They don't bring her food, but a menu. She decides whether she wants pancakes or eggs, and while the kids and her husband cook, she lounges in bed drinking coffee and reading. When it's time to eat, she joins them downstairs, and receives flowers and homemade cards.

Role Reversal

For a full day, have your kids mother you. They can pick out your clothes, cook your breakfast, kiss your boo-boos, read you a story, and tuck you in bed at the end of the day. You'll probably also get some lollypops and new toys.

Queen for a Day

Remember the old television show *Queen for a Day*? Get the kids and your husband prepared in advance to bow down to your commands, and get a robe and tiara ready. Have them give you flowers when they put on your robe and crown, then have an "audience" with them while they tell you just why they think you are a royally spectacular mother. It's also important that they prepare a feast, and that you don't do any dishes or laundry all day.

Mother Wisdom

If you're like most mothers, there are probably a handful of sayings and certain types of practical advice (also called nagging) for which you are known. Your husband or an older child can get each of the kids to write on sheets of letter-sized paper something they've learned from you that's proved valuable, or something they promise to pay more attention to in the future. The sheets can be stapled together in a sort of book.

Father's Day

A T-Shirt to Melt His Heart

Materials

White cotton t-shirt; fabric paints in one or more bright colors; paintbrush.

Instructions

Pour some paint into a shallow foil baking pan, and have your kids place either the palms of their hands or their feet into the paint. Have them make a print of their hands or feet on the front of the t-shirt, and write next to the prints either "I'm in good hands with Dad" or "I want to walk in Dad's footsteps." If you have more than one child, you can change the wording to "We're in good hands," etc. Have them wash all the paint off their skin immediately. Tiny baby feet and hands are adorable mementos, but you can make this an annual tradition, a clever way to chart the kids' growth.

The McCandless family of Philadelphia has an annual "Guy Day" on Father's Day, which is a series of special events for all the guys in the extended family, little boys included. The women plan and pay for a day of adventure, which may include tickets to a local air show, touring a naval shipyard, or visiting a train museum. The women and girls stay home and prepare a picnic supper.

July 4
A "Happy Birthday, America" Party

Food

Serve typical barbecue fare such as hot dogs or chicken, and be sure to include a cake with white frosting, topped with strawberries and blueberries. Instead of regular candles, use sparklers if you have them.

Music

Get a CD with Sousa marches and patriotic favorites, or lead a singalong of "Yankee Doodle Dandy," "America the Beautiful," and others. Provide printouts of the lyrics (**www.patrioticon.org/patriotic-sound files lyrics.htm**). Be sure to sing "Happy Birthday, America" before lighting the sparklers or candles and cutting the cake.

Party Hats

You could use construction paper to fashion hats, such as Uncle Sam's stovepipe hat, in red, white, and blue. Just make a cylinder of paper about 8 inches high, glue the edges so it fits the child's head, and cut a matching brim. (Cut it extra wide so there's paper you can tuck and glue to the bottom of the hat. No need to worry about a top.) Or, you could use green paper and make some simple Statue of Liberty hats, just a crown shape with spikes sticking up. Your local party store will also stock hats.

Activities

Read aloud from the Declaration of Independence. Although the long list of complaints about George III gets boring, the initial section is very inspiring. "We hold these truths to be self-evident, that all men are created equal" and so on. Borrowing from the Jewish tradition of thinking about the importance and joy of freedom, have everyone at the table talk about why they value freedom, and what life is like today in countries whose citizens are not free.

Patriotic Websites

To read the Declaration of Independence, go to **www.ushistory.org/declaration/** which will give you not only that document, but also the backgrounds of its signers and many useful links to related sites.

An educational website with patriotic craft ideas such as flag flowerpots and star necklaces is **www.enchantedlearning.com/crafts/patriotic.**

all men are created equal

Halloween

What is now called Halloween has its roots in ancient Celtic celebrations of New Year's: October 31 was the last day of summer in the ancient Irish calendar. People believed that on this day, the barrier between the worlds of living and dead got thin, and the spirits of the dead could walk among the living. To frighten away those spirits, the villagers would dress in ghoulish costumes and party loudly. Another ancient Celtic tradition was to ritually cast out all the evil from the year just ending, to prepare for a good new year. It was the latter tradition that inspired Lucinda Herring to create the unusual ritual that follows.

Gloom Dolls: A Healing Activity for Halloween

Materials
Paper; pencils or crayons; white cloth cut into squares measuring 12 inches by 12 inches (you can use an old sheet); newspapers or wood; matches, to make a fire.

Instructions
Have each person write his or her "glooms" on pieces of paper. These are things and feelings that family members don't like about their lives, from not making the soccer team to a serious illness or other crisis in the family. Unless the children need someone to write for them or want to share their glooms, these should be private. After the glooms are written down, crumble the paper into a ball. This will be the doll's head. Stick it in the middle of the fabric square, then use a piece of string to tie the fabric around the balled-up paper, thus forming a head. In a fireplace inside or a grill outside, start a small fire. Talk about letting go of all the bad feelings that "haunt" us. Then everybody throws their gloom dolls into the fire and watches them burn.

More Fun Halloween Ideas

Harvest Festival

Families that wish to steer clear of gory, scary Halloween celebrations can follow the example of the Gines family of Michigan. They celebrate the month of October as a continuous harvest festival. One weekend, they take a hayride at a local orchard, and pick their own apples and pumpkins. One week, they make a scarecrow as a family. And one weekend they make "suncatchers:" They collect fall leaves, grasses, and flowers and lay them down on waxed paper, then shred crayons on top of the paper, cover it with a second layer, and then iron the waxed paper till the crayons melt. They cut the paper into circles and other shapes, poke a hole in the top, and hang their suncatchers around the kitchen, to catch the fall light.

> ### Halloween Website
>
> www.halloweenmagazine.com is an excellent site with tons of links for stories and crafts, and an online quiz that teaches kids safety tips for trick-or-treating.

Ghoulish Fun

Kyna Tabor of Salem, Illinois, takes her kids to a nearby graveyard every Halloween day to make grave rubbings. This particular graveyard dates to the Civil War, and many of the graves are old, with interesting markings. She uses butcher's paper, which you can get from your local supermarket, and either charcoal or sidewalk chalk. If your kids are older, you can sit around in the dark, with only the light of candles (in or out of carved pumpkins), and take turns telling ghost stories.

> ### How to Toast Pumpkin Seeds
>
> Separate seeds from strings and toss with a spoonful of vegetable oil. Spread seeds across a cookie sheet and sprinkle with salt. Bake at 250° for 90 minutes to dry, then raise heat to 350° to toast. Done when lightly brown.

Thanksgiving

How to Make a Thankfulness Tree

Materials

Construction paper in red, yellow, and orange; pencil; scissors; string; bare tree branches about 2 to 3 feet long; vase for branches.

Instructions

Trace the maple leaf shape on this page, or draw a template of your own. Once you have the template, use a pencil and outline the leaf shape on the colored paper. Cut out as many leaf shapes as you wish. If your children are very young, you may want to do this part ahead. Spread the leaves across the table, and let everybody in the family write things on the leaves for which they are thankful that year. Poke a small hole in the stem part of the leaves, thread with string, and hang on the branches. Afterwards, save all the leaves, either gluing them into the family scrapbook or stuffing them in a plastic baggy marked with the year. (When he gets older, my son will love that he was thankful for "my brane" at age six.)

Alternative Idea

Make your thankfulness tree as a poster, drawing a picture of a tree, then having the kids trace around their hands on colored paper and make those handprints the leaves. Glue "leaves" to tree on poster.

More Ideas for Giving Thanks

The core emotional truth of Thanksgiving is the expression of gratitude, and the best model for kids is a joyful tradition of giving thanks.

Thankful Box

Put a cardboard box with a slit cut into the top on the kitchen counter the week before Thanksgiving, with a pile of blank paper and a pencil next to it. Everybody writes down things they're thankful for. Read them aloud during the feast, and guess who wrote what.

Thanksgiving Scroll

Each year before the feast, the Butman family of Walkersville, Maryland, unrolls a paper scroll across the kitchen table. (Arts and crafts stores sell paper rolls, which are about 1 foot wide.) To start, Bryan Butman or one of his three kids picks out a Bible verse having to do with giving thanks, and they write it across the top. The paper is taped to the table and divided into five sections, one for each family member. Each family member draws or colors something they were thankful for that year, whether a pet, good grades, or close friends. The Butmans keep adding on to the same scroll until it's full, but you could also cut off each year's section and carefully tape it to the dining room wall while eating your feast.

Corn Kernels

Put three kernels of corn next to each place setting for Thanksgiving dinner, and at some point, have each person count out three things for which they are grateful.

Thank-You Notes

Kim Meisenheimer realized that many of the people for whom her kids were thankful didn't come to their Thanksgiving dinner. So she started having her sons write (and mail) two or three special thank-you notes a year to special people, anyone from the soccer coach to Grandma. On Thanksgiving Day itself, each family member could be required to write a thank-you note to each other person attending the feast. Slip them under the plates before the meal.

Connecting When You're Apart

On the day before Thanksgiving, Gines family members all over the country make pie at exactly the same time, using Grandma Betty's pie crust recipe. Betty herself calls each household in turn, and speaks to each grandchild.

Fun Thanksgiving Dinner Ideas

Autograph the Tablecloth

In Mindy Robinson's family, 30 or 40 people attended the feast, and every person signed the tablecloth with a pen during dinner. Afterward, her mother would embroider around the names, in a different color thread each year. (The year was embroidered around the edge of the tablecloth, in the color used that year.) The cloth became a visual history of the holiday, reminding the family who was missing this year and how much the little ones grew, as signatures changed.

Kid-Friendly Feast

Monica Hall of Baltimore got tired of cranky kids forced to sit too long. She puts the little ones at a separate table, buys extra turkey legs, and gives them cranberry Jell-O® instead of cranberry sauce. When they finish, they can play in the basement playroom while the adults converse.

Turkey Parade

One family finds that once all the dishes are finally ready, they need to let off some steam and stretch their legs before sitting down to eat. Each person attending is given a pot or pan and a spoon, and the cook carries the finished turkey on a large platter. The group literally parades down the street (briefly, before the bird cools completely) banging on pots and screaming "Happy Thanksgiving!" to the neighborhood.

Pilgrims and Indians

Allison Dafferner's family had a tradition of making Pilgrim and Indian hats. It gave the kids something to do while her mother cooked, and it sure was festive. The hats are made from colored construction paper and glued or stapled together. Tradition has it that the kids pick first whether they want to be Pilgrims or Indians, and the adults, who also participate, balance out the numbers.

Thanksgiving Website

To research the authentic history of Thanksgiving and also look up a good grace to say before the feast, you won't do better than **www.night.net/thanksgiving/first.html-ssi**.

Sharing the Bounty of Thanksgiving

This is a great holiday to start philanthropic traditions and link gratitude with sharing.

Make a Helping Others Jar

Take a used, clean coffee can and cut a slit in the plastic top. To decorate the can, cut white paper the height of the can, wrap this paper around the can, and secure with glue or tape. To decorate, use crayons or markers, or paste magazine photos on the paper. Display the can in the kitchen, and put some money in while discussing a weekly plan of family giving. Talk about how that money could help others and discuss possible charities.

Feast for the Animals

Nancy Mendez and her family share their feast with "the birds and beasts." Before they eat, her children and their cousins take a walk in the nearby woods (with a grown-up), carrying a bucket of seeds and food scraps. On the way back home, the kids fill the bucket with twigs and kindling for the fireplace.

Feed the Poor

Some families try to work some part of the Thanks-giving weekend in a soup kitchen, but there are other ways you can help as well. One is to buy a duplicate feast: If you're having turkey, buy a second bird; if you're making mashed potatoes, buy a second bag. Pack this feast and deliver it to a local homeless shelter or agency that serves the poor. (Make this arrangement before buying the food.)

A Great Charity for Kids

Heifer International has over 50 years experience in donating farm animals to the world's poor, and has a great website, **www.heifer.org**. Also, the picture book *Beatrice's Goat*, about how a heifer goat changed the life of a real African girl, makes a big impression on kids.

Hanukkah

Just as many Christian families are trying to lessen the materialistic aspects of Christmas, many Jewish families emphasize meaning over gifts. Here are some Hanukkah celebration ideas:

Theme Nights

The Elkins of Boston used to give their kids a present each of the eight nights of Hanukkah, just as they had been given nightly gifts as children. But Judy Elkin and her husband decided that with three kids, the practice was expensive and not sending the right message. Now, the kids get a gift from their parents every other night. On the first night, the kids only get gifts from each other; one night is "family fun night" featuring an activity like bowling; and one night is *tzedaka*, or charity, night. Every Friday, before their Shabbat dinner, the family has put aside money for charity, and on this night, they decide on who should get the donation.

Focus on Food

Ellen Brosbe tries to emphasize the food, which is fried in honor of the miraculous oil that burned for eight days. Her kids take turns picking the menu: one night it's fish and chips, another night tempura, and so on. Instead of gifts, her kids get money, one dollar multiplied by the number of candles lit each night.

Hanukkah Websites

Produced by an organization of observant Jews, www.virtualchanukah.com is rich in history and activities. There are stories, prayers, and a feature called "Share a Mitzvah," where people can record a good deed they have done.

A less religious approach is at www.child fun.com/themes/han.shtml, whose crafts and activities include making a menorah of Play Doh®.

How to Play Dreidel

A dreidel is a top with four sides, and each side has a Hebrew letter. Together, they stand for the phrase "A great miracle happened there." Some families play for pennies, while others use nuts or candy. First, the pennies or treats are divided evenly among the players. Each person puts one piece in a central pot or cup, perhaps two if the group is small. Players take turns spinning the dreidel and react according to what symbol is facing up:

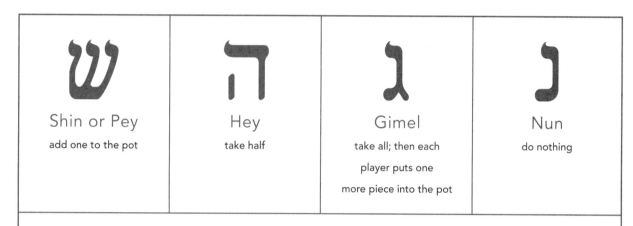

ש	**ה**	**ג**	**נ**
Shin or Pey	Hey	Gimel	Nun
add one to the pot	take half	take all; then each player puts one more piece into the pot	do nothing

Dreidel song

The song is called "I Have a Little Dreidel." One place to go if you don't know the tune is **www.night.net/kids/hanukkah-dreidel.html.**

I have a little dreidel,

I made it out of clay,

And when it's dry and ready,

That dreidel I shall play.

chorus: Oh dreidel, dreidel, dreidel,

I made it out of clay:

Oh dreidel, dreidel, dreidel,

Now dreidel I shall play....

Winter Solstice

The shortest day of the year, which varies between December 21 and 22, has been celebrated for centuries by many diverse cultures. Traditional celebrations usually include fire, light, and quiet contemplation.

Family Solstice Celebrations

Solstice Dinner

Jeanne Mollinger-Lewis's family has a special dinner emphasizing "food the sun grows," like nuts and fruit, and the kids get a major gift on this day. They line the walk to their front door with luminarias (candles inside paper bags weighted down with sand), and light sparklers and small fireworks they've saved from July 4.

Solstice Wreath

Rain Mako, who lives in a cabin in the Ozarks with her husband and children, makes a wreath from a long, bare grapevine she finds near their property. To decorate it for solstice, the family cuts evergreen boughs and inserts them in the twisted wreath, and adds tiny white lights. Rain always felt her kids weren't grateful for the pile of gifts they got on Christmas, so her sons now get one present a day between winter solstice and Christmas, left near the wreath.

Not sure what day to celebrate solstice, or when Hanukkah falls this year? *Chase's Calendar of Events* , a book carried by most public libraries, lists a wide range of holidays and historical events. It's updated every year.

Pre-Christmas: Celebrate the Whole Month

St. Nicholas Day

December 6 is the day many countries celebrate a bishop who became a saint and was said to rescue children and help the poor. Once her kids were old enough, Teresa Schultz-Jones started the tradition that St. Nicholas leaves craft kits for each of them, so they can make gifts for others.

Good Deed Paper Chain

Sara Tapley, the mother of six, hangs a multicolored paper chain across the bay window in her dining room, after writing the name of one family member on each link. Every morning, each person has to break a link and do a good deed for the person whose name he gets; if someone gets their own name, he passes it on.

Manger Rituals

The Schroeder family has 16 characters in its nativity set, and all except baby Jesus are wrapped up before the holidays begin. Each night after dinner, the kids take turns picking one wrapped character and setting it into the manger scene. That child then gets to pick which Christmas carol the family sings that night. Baby Jesus doesn't get put into the manger until Christmas morning, when the family sings "Happy Birthday, Jesus." Another family sets up its wise men across the room from the nativity scene, and every day of Advent moves them slightly closer.

Christmas Box

In the Gardiner family, the two daughters each have a pretty Christmas tin reserved for them, always kept on a certain windowsill during December. Every morning, they run to their tins to see what treat they got that day: it could be candy, a Christmas poem, a puzzle, or tickets to the *Nutcracker* ballet.

Make Your Own Advent Calendar

There are hundreds of commercial versions, but it's easy to make your own.

Materials

Felt fabric, in black, red, green, and yellow. Buy a yard of black felt, and a half yard each of red, green, and yellow. Scissors, fabric marker, and fabric glue. Dowel rod about half an inch in diameter, or less, cut to a length of 24 inches.

Instructions

The black felt is the background. Cut it to be 19 inches wide and 35 inches high. Cut the pockets 3 inches by 3 inches, and cut 12 pockets of red felt and 12 pockets of green. Cut three stars out of the yellow felt, one bigger than the other two. Next, lay all the pieces on the black background, leaving two inches empty at the top. There are six rows of four pockets, and they should alternate between red and green. There should be about an inch between the pockets. Number the pockets, 1 to 24. This can be done using glitter and glue or by cutting out the numbers from the yellow felt. If using felt numbers, glue them on using fabric glue. Glue the pockets (or sew if you prefer) to the background—remember to just secure three edges and leave the top open! Attach the stars in a row at the top, with the big one in the middle.

To hang, roll the top inch and a half of the black felt to the back, creating a sleeve through which you can insert the dowel rod. Glue or sew the edge to the back, to secure it. The rod will stick out at both ends, and you can hang the calendar on two nails, or if you wish, tie a ribbon to both ends of the rod and hang, using the ribbon, on one nail.

The Ritual

Starting on December 1, put something special in a pocket each day: it could be a piece of candy, a Bible verse, a small toy, or a combination of these.

How to Make an Advent Wreath

"Advent" comes from the Latin word for coming, and many Christians find that using the full month before Christmas to concentrate on the religious meaning of this holiday helps to counteract the materialistic messages that bombard kids.

Materials

A simple Styrofoam wreath shape from the local craft store (a donut shape); plastic pine boughs or live ones from your yard; five candles, either three purple and one pink or four purple, plus one white (though in a pinch, any color will do); a simple holder for one candle.

Instructions

Stick the purple and pink candles into the Styrofoam, roughly at what would be the "corners" of the wreath. Then stick the pine boughs in all the way around the wreath, covering the white base. Decorate further, if you wish, with red ribbon, which can also be glued in a band around the base if the white Styrofoam shows through the greens. The fourth candle, the white one, goes into the holder, which is placed on your table inside the wreath. The greens are symbolic of new life and hope, while the flames stand for the light of Christ: the closer we get to his birth, the greater the light.

The Ritual

The first week's candle (purple) stands for hope; the second (purple) stands for love; the third (pink) for joy; and the fourth (purple) means peace. The fifth (white), which goes in the center and is lighted on Christmas Eve, is the Christ candle. On the first Sunday, light just the first candle: on the second light the first and the second, and so on. If you light candles each night, add a new candle on Sunday. Many families read a Bible passage after lighting candles. An excellent source of daily Bible readings and meditations is Alternatives for Simple Living's annual booklet "Whose Birthday Is It, Anyway?" (**www.simpleliving.org** or 800-821-6153).

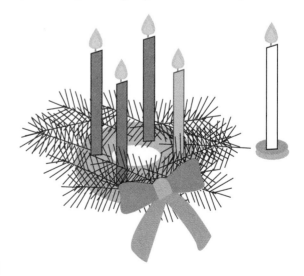

More Family Christmas Celebrations

Christmas Reading Rituals

Literary Advent Calendar

Take every holiday-related book you have and wrap them in Christmas paper. Write a number from 1 to 24 on the front of each package. If you don't have 24 books, use a few from the library before they're due, cut out a Christmas story from a magazine, or wrap a video. We save *The Night Before Christmas* for Christmas Eve. Every evening after supper, I place a book under a felt Advent calendar hanging on a doorknob in the playroom. My son takes an ornament from a numbered pocket and puts it on the felt tree; then he gets to open the day's book. To keep these books special, I pack them away in a box in the attic after the holiday. This is one of my son's favorite rituals. I got it from Nancy Giehl of Boulder, Colorado, who read it in *Family Fun* magazine (which has great ritual ideas every month—call 800-289-4849 to subscribe).

Night Tree

The Brock family loves this holiday book by Eve Bunting, which is based on an actual family's Christmas ritual. The family in the book visits the same pine tree in the woods near their town each year on Christmas Eve, and they decorate it with treats for birds and other wildlife. The Brocks follow the ritual pretty closely, but do it in a wooded area on their property in Cheney, Washington. Beforehand, they make a garland of cranberries and breakfast cereal (popcorn works too), and roll pinecones in birdseed after slathering them with peanut butter. After decorating the tree together, they sing carols and drink hot chocolate from a thermos.

More Great Christmas Books

There are classics like *The Night Before Christmas*, but here are some lesser-known books my son loves:

- 🎄 *The Polar Express* by Chris Van Allsburg
- 🎄 *The Christmas Miracle of Jonathan Toomey* by Susan Wojciechowski
- 🎄 *December* by Eve Bunting
- 🎄 *Olive, the Other Reindeer* by J. Otto Seibold and Vivian Walsh

Camp Christmas

One winter when she had 16 family members coming to visit her in Texas for the holidays and a limited amount of funds, Mary Kay Havens and her daughter created "Camp Christmas." They chose the word "camp" to suggest informality (sleeping bags and all) and fun, group activities. The highlight was a group carriage ride around Dallas followed by a candlelight church service, but much of the time was spent at the Havens house, doing things in shifts. One small group would bake cookies while another sang carols and a third decorated Santa hats.

Candle Night

On Christmas Eve after church, the Straw family lights every candle they own. They read the Christmas story from the Bible, and eat Christmas cookies with milk. The Taylor family of New Bedford, Massachusetts, has a different candle ritual that night: Sitting around the tree, each person is given an unlit candle. A lighted candle is on a table nearby. The first person lights his or her candle, tells about a prayer that God answered in the past year, then asks for help with something else. He or she lights the candle of the next person, who does the same, and so on. When all the candles are lit, the family sings carols and the youngest puts Jesus in the manger under the tree.

Hark the herald angels sing

Journey to Bethlehem

In Nevada, the Hiltons pretend one night to follow in the footsteps of Mary and Joseph. They troop through the house and yard, as though on a journey, winding up at the foot of their Christmas tree. By candlelight, they have a picnic on a blanket, eating foods Mary and Joseph may have had such as pita bread, fruit, and nuts.

Christmas Gift Rituals

One way to add meaning to the holiday is to give fewer gifts, but make the giving of them part of the ritual.

Three Gifts

Some families give each of their kids only three gifts, explaining that Jesus received three gifts from the wise men, and why should anyone else get more?

The Suk family of Evanston, Illinois, follows this practice, but creatively. Each child gets one book, one game, and one toy, usually something major like a bicycle or electric guitar. The little things are wrapped and under the tree, but the major gifts are hidden, and the kids have to solve clues to find them. One year, the clues led to a garage-door opener, which led to a neighbor's garage and the hidden bike. The whole family troops around together as each child searches, youngest first.

Goofy Slippers

Pam Pinegar, a self-described "small woman with big feet," started a tradition with her two daughters that each year they buy one another the goofiest slippers they can find. Theme presents are fun, and many families give their kids new, Christmas-themed pajamas on Christmas Eve (at least no one looks ratty for the family photos).

Great Christmas Websites

Extensive resources for a religious Christmas observance are found at **www.rockies.net/~spirit/sermons/christmas page.html.**

Another good site for Christians is Christmas in Cyberspace, which can be found at **www.njwebworks.net/christmas/.**

For lots of fun activities, **www.Christmas.com** is loaded with options. Click on "spirit" in the menu, under "entertainment," and you'll find recipes, carols, prayers, and even a list of published Christmas plays.

Gift Exchange

One way to limit excess is to pick names out of a hat, so extended family members have to shop for only one person. The Trieschman family of Baltimore picks names on Thanksgiving, and add to the fun by delivering a "joke gift" to the person between that holiday and Christmas. They try to do it anonymously and make it as silly as possible: Cindy Trieschman actually rented a donkey for a day, and snuck it into her father's tool shed. On Christmas, the adults don't get to open their regular present until they accurately guess who picked their name.

Kwanzaa

Introduced in 1966, Kwanzaa is a celebration of African culture that runs from the day after Christmas through New Year's Day. Each day is devoted to a different principle. More and more cities have public Kwanzaa celebrations, but many African-American families also observe the holiday at home.

Some Family-Style Kwanzaa Celebrations

Candle Ceremony

A basic part of Kwanzaa is lighting candles each night, and talking about the principle of the day. In Washington, D.C., Yvette Aidara, mother of a teenage son, celebrates with a group of friends, who take turns hosting on successive evenings. Among the children present, a different one is chosen each night to say the name of the day's principle in English and Swahili. Then, each person in the group says how they will put that principle into practice in the coming year.

Creativity Party

Many families hold a party during the week of Kwanzaa around a particular theme. Angela Dodson and Michael Days in Trenton, New Jersey, usually choose the theme of creativity. Guests perform, telling stories or reading poems, and each brings to the feast a dish that has African origins.

History Game

Retelling history, particularly of one's ancestors, is another important part of Kwanzaa, and the Ruff family of Dublin, Ohio, always includes a history game in its annual New Year's Eve party. In one game, the names of famous Africans are pinned on the backs of some guests, and they ask questions of others until they guess the name pinned to them. Those who are able to celebrate Kwanzaa with much of their extended families favor oral history projects such as getting the children to tape record interviews with their grandparents.

Kwanzaa Website

The Kwanzaa Information Center includes recommended books, ideas for family ceremonies, and message boards. Go to www.melanet.com/kwanzaa.

Kwanzaa for Beginners: Lighting the Candles
How to Make a Kinara, or Kwanzaa Candleholder

Materials

(You can use any recipe for nontoxic clay. This one comes from the Klutz guide *Arts and Crafts Recipes*.) 2 cups baking soda, 1 cup cornstarch, 1¼ cups cold water, paints, paintbrush, seven candles: three red, three green, and one black.

Instructions

Mix the baking soda and cornstarch in a saucepan. Add water. Cook the mixture over medium-high heat, stirring constantly until it's the consistency of mashed potatoes. Spoon dough onto a plate and cover with a damp cloth to cool. When cool, roll the clay into seven balls and attach them side-by-side. Stick the candles into the balls, then pull them out to leave seven holes. The clay will take up to two days to dry; then you can paint your kinara. You might want to use the Kwanzaa colors of red, green, and black.

Activity

Place the black candle, for the African people, in the center, with the three green candles (for young people) and the three red ones (for struggle), on either side of it. The first night, light just the black candle and discuss the first principle, unity. The next night, light the black candle and one other and discuss the second principle, and so on, as follows: Second night, self-determination. Third night, collective work and responsibility. Fourth night, cooperative economics. Fifth night, purpose. Sixth night, creativity. Last night, faith.

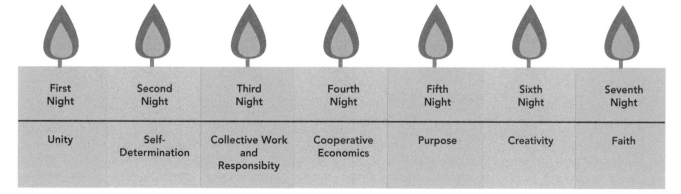

First Night	Second Night	Third Night	Fourth Night	Fifth Night	Sixth Night	Seventh Night
Unity	Self-Determination	Collective Work and Responsibity	Cooperative Economics	Purpose	Creativity	Faith

Family Festivities and Ceremonies

Birthdays

Everything Balloons

One of the best ways to celebrate birthdays is with balloons, which are not only a perfect symbol for the pumped-up excitement of a kid on this day, but are also incredibly versatile.

Chairs and Beds

Get a bouquet of helium balloons and tie them to your child's chair at dinner to designate the "birthday girl" or "birthday boy." Or, tie a Mylar or a helium balloon to the end of their bed after they fall asleep (it must be Mylar to last overnight; a regular balloon filled with helium will sink by morning).

How to Make a Balloon Tunnel

Ron Greenberg celebrates the birthdays of his daughters by constructing a "balloon tunnel" on the stairs. When the birthday girl awakes, she must be the first one to squeeze into the tunnel, slide downstairs on her backside, and pick up the wrapped present at the bottom, her first of the day.

Ron starts with about 50 helium balloons, which are tied to the banisters on one side or the other with ribbons. Half are tied to one side of the banister, and half to the other, and they are criss-crossed in the middle. Because the helium holds them up, there is plenty of room for kids (and adults) to slide underneath them, but not enough room to stand. To close it off and give it more of a tunnel feeling and look, Ron threads crepe-paper streamers through and around the ribbons holding the balloons.

Balloon Countdown

As toddlers, her kids constantly asked, "How many days till my birthday?" so Debbie Midcalf created a balloon ritual for counting down the days. A week or so before the birthday, she blows up balloons, one for each day, and hangs them on a string across the dining room. All the balloons are the same color, except the last one, which represents the actual birthday. Every day her child gets to pop one balloon, and count how many are left.

Balloon Forest

A great way to decorate your dining room for a birthday feast is to get 25 or 30 regular balloons, in bright colors, inflated with helium. When you get them home, separate the ribbons and let the balloons bounce up to the ceiling. Keep the ribbons long, just reaching to the top of the table, so you have to look at each other through a forest of ribbons. An ordinary room becomes magical.

Balloon Wishes

After blowing out candles, take your child outside with three helium-filled balloons. Let him or her make three wishes and, as they silently make each wish, let go of one balloon.

Great Birthday Celebrations

Giving Instead of Getting

The Hassells of Winterport, Maine, wanted to cultivate a generous impulse in their kids, and started the ritual that on a person's birthday, they buy gifts for everyone else. They still get a special dinner and cake with candles (plus presents from grandparents and friends). They also look forward to their siblings' birthdays, knowing they'll get presents on each of those occasions. Mary Bliss Hassell says kids get used to anything if that's all they know; she began this practice when the youngest was a toddler.

Celebrate Growth

Gertrud Mueller Nelson, author of *To Dance with God: Family Ritual and Community Celebration*, gave her kids two envelopes on their birthdays. One was marked "New Privilege" and the other "New Responsibility." A child turning six might be given the privilege of staying up an extra half hour at night, and the responsibility of feeding the dog its dinner. This ritual "gave them a sense of importance and made them feel grown up," says Gertrud.

Memorable Birthday Photos

When her daughter turned one year old, novelist Jean Hanff Korelitz got the idea of photographing Dorothy in a dress that had belonged to her own mother. Every year on Dorothy's birthday, Jean takes more pictures of Dorothy in "the dress," and each year, it comes closer to actually fitting. The photo sessions are full of clowning and silly poses, and the pictures have been compiled into collages that line one staircase. When her son celebrated his first birthday, Jean started the birthday photography tradition for him, shooting Asher in a white dress shirt of his father's.

Stuffed Animal Parade

When my son comes home from school on his birthday, his stuffed animals line the staircase to the second floor, on both sides. When he gets to the top, he finds his first present of the day.

More Birthday Celebrations

Birthday Wreaths

In a ritual she says was inspired by Navajo traditions to celebrate a newborn, Kathleen Metcalf gave each of her children a simple wreath from a craft store when they were infants. The idea is that each year, friends and family give the birthday child a small charm or object to attach to the wreath that symbolizes something special about that year, or a positive attribute of their character. A special diary records each little gift as it is added, its significance, and who gave it. The wreaths hang in the children's bedrooms, and are now quite crowded with little objects that tell the stories of their lives. In addition, the birthday kid gets one big gift, "usually something useful, like a sleeping bag," says Kathleen.

Boss of the Family

In one family, the birthday boy or girl is "boss for the day" and can order other family members around. They decide on the day's menu and activities, and usually send their parents to bed early!

Make Way for New Toys

Before her daughters' birthdays, Barbara Franco of Florida gets them to help in a major cleanup ritual that includes donating old toys they no longer play with to a local shelter or other charity. Clothes are also sorted through, and those that don't fit are passed on to the next youngest, or donated to the poor.

Great Books on Themed Parties

There's a dinosaur party, mystery party, and more in *The Kids' Pick-a-Party Book: 50 Fun Party Themes for Kids, Ages 2 to 16* by Penny Warner.

There are 90 themed parties in *Clever Party Planning: Ideas and Themes for Kids, Teens and Adults* by Suzanne Singleton.

More party ideas can be found at **www.familyfun.com**, and in the book, *Family Fun Parties*.

Milestone Birthdays

How to Make a Threshold Sheet

When my son, Max, turned three, it felt like a special milestone to me and I wanted to find a creative way to celebrate his new powers. I thought about tribal rites of passage, where those initiated into a new stage have to cross over a physical threshold and bravely face the adventure of their future. I decided I could make a threshold with a simple sheet. Max would have to go through the sheet to get his birthday gifts, and I could use the blank surface to record his accomplishments. I painted symbols of "big boyness" on the first sheet, including underwear, since he had just been potty-trained, and scissors, to symbolize nursery school.

I've since made two more threshold sheets, one when he turned five, and another at seven. At five, the sheet was painted like a pirate's treasure map. At seven, it was a list of breakthrough achievements like "Max can read," "Max can write," and "Max can swim." He loves these sheets.

Materials

One white, full-size bedsheet; washable paint in bright colors, plus black; pencil; scissors; newspaper.

Instructions

Put plenty of newspaper on the floor to protect from stains. Spread the sheet out flat. Cut a slit from the bottom to the middle, ending slightly higher than the child is tall. Sketch your design in pencil first, then paint. Let dry completely before handling. On the big day, use masking tape to hang sheet across a doorway that leads to the room where the presents are.

More Ideas for Milestone Birthdays

Ideas vary from family to family about what is a milestone birthday. Is it reaching 10, the first double-digit year? Or 12? Or the first teen year, magical 13?

The most meaningful celebrations come from deep personal knowledge of a particular child, and his or her dreams and aspirations. When my little sister turned 16, I happened to know she had "never been kissed" so I assembled half a dozen boys from my high school class, who lined up to kiss her during a slumber party. She still thinks it was the best ritual I ever did.

Milestone Gifts

In the Chesto family, you get your own alarm clock at age 10, symbolizing that you have the maturity to rouse yourself in the morning and get ready for school without being nagged. Jeff Butler gives his kids, boys and girls, a Swiss Army knife at 10, proof they can take care of themselves and have good judgment in a crisis. The ritual includes going out to dinner alone with Dad, and picking out the exact right model of knife.

Milestone Trips

For families that love the outdoors, a birthday that signals maturity might be the time for the first white-river rafting trip with Mom and Dad. Or the first night for a sleepaway with friends in the family's vacation cabin (with the parents staying a cell phone call away). Or the first time to try climbing to the summit of the closest challenging mountain.

Upon completion of the physical challenge, a good gift might be a keepsake of the accomplishment, like a key chain inscribed with the date.

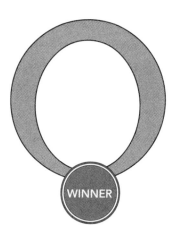

Medals Ceremony

If this has been a year of big accomplishments, like learning to read, make some medals for your child out of gold paper and wide, blue ribbon. Write the accomplishment, or just "winner" on the medal, and ceremonially drape it around the birthday kid's neck.

Half Birthdays

With children, the amount of change and growth that occurs in just six months can be astonishing. Celebrating half birthdays is a way to acknowledge and honor that growth.

Half a Cake

Patrice Kyger says her kids love it that she notices how much they change in half a year. For their half birthdays, there are no gifts or parties, but her kids get half a cake (she freezes the rest) and one candle. And they get to pick the menu for dinner.

Half a Song

There are several ways to halve the classic birthday song. You can sing "Happy Half Birthday to You!" or you could try only singing every other word.

Half a Game

Doni Boyd's kids were both born in January, so she always threw them a joint half birthday party in July, making it as silly as possible. "We would put the picnic table half in our yard, and half in the neighbor's yard," she explains. "I would serve half a cake, and cut ice cream bars in half. Since it was summer, everybody would come half dressed." To increase the fun, people brought only half a present (the board for a game, but not the game pieces, which would be saved for another time), and played half games. "Everybody loved the idea of letting the kids go hide, but no one would go seeking them!" says Doni.

Treats at Breakfast or Lunch

Since many family birthdays involve special dinners, confine the special treats to breakfast. Give the half birthday child a cupcake or special muffin with one candle. Or, send an extra-special desert in her lunchbox that day, with a very small birthday card.

Star Birthdays

A star birthday, sometimes called a golden birthday, is when someone's birthday date and age are the same, like being seven on June 7. It doesn't always happen in childhood, but it is a once-in-a-lifetime thing, and some families love to honor that rarity.

Stars Everywhere

Some feel the best decoration for this day is stars, and that there can't be too many of them. Patrice Kyger decorates her whole house with shiny star garlands, wrapping them around picture frames, lamps, and furniture. She also buys star-shaped candles, and sprinkles stars all over the birthday cake. You could also make this a day to visit the nearest planetarium "star show," or let the birthday kid stay up late and look at the stars outside your home.

Star Treatment

Give the birthday child the total movie star treatment. If it's a girl, this could include a beauty makeover at the local beauty parlor or a special gift of age-appropriate beauty products. If it's a boy, get a costume for a spaceman or safari guide, and photograph him in heroic poses. Make a movie of the whole day, featuring your star. You could write a script in advance about the history of their life and success, "up from humble beginnings," or they could help write it. Make sure you include an on-camera interview with the star, about their tips on life. Ask for their autograph often.

Star Gifts

Some families give the child with a star birthday the number of presents equivalent to their age. But if a 10-year-old is getting 10 gifts, only one will be something big and the rest will be tokens and trinkets. Wrap each one, even the smallest, in the biggest boxes you have, and tape a big number on the side or top of each package. Save the best for last, so you build up to it at the climax.

Adoption Days

Many parents of adopted children celebrate the anniversary of the day they adopted a child as well as his or her birthday. It's a way of honoring sometimes complicated roots, and celebrating the act of love in welcoming this child into this family.

Homecoming Day

The Hoddinott family celebrates the adoption days of two children born in Korea, but is sensitive to the feelings of a biological daughter. "To us, it's a way to keep the door open, to allow them to ask questions and hear their stories over and over," says Julie Hoddinott. "It's obvious they're adopted because they don't look like us, and it's important to acknowledge their histories." The family has a special desert on Homecoming Day, but it's important to Julie that the cake is shared by all. On each boy's Homecoming Day, she shows the video taken the day he arrived from Korea, and the family looks at baby pictures from that time.

Family Day

A couple in Minnesota adopted two Romanian orphans in 1991, and decided to celebrate the adoptions on an annual day called Family Day. At a festive dinner, they retell the story of the adoptions, but also take time to talk about a biological daughter who committed suicide in her teens. There are five candles on the cake, including one for this girl. The message this family hopes to communicate is a hopeful one, that no matter what, once a person joins this family, they are part of it forever, and everybody's story matters.

Talking to a Star

When Lucy Steinitz noticed that her daughter, adopted as an infant from Guatemala, got sad on her birthdays, wondering about the mother that let her go, Lucy invented a special birthday ritual. She told Elsita she didn't know much about the woman, but suggested, "If you look out your bedroom window and talk to a star, and tell her what she needs to know about you, I just know she'll be listening." The ritual always made Elsita feel better, and as a teenager, Lucy took her for a "cultural heritage" trip to Guatemala.

School Days

Preparing First-Timers

The beginning of preschool is one of the biggest transitions your children will ever go through, at an age when change is especially scary. Preparing them well and making the send-off a joyful ritual will equip them well for all the transitions ahead.

Meet the Teacher/ Playground Picnic

Most preschools arrange a tour of the school to acclimate the new kids. Take advantage of it, and try to engage your child in a conversation with the teacher. Take your camera and take a photo of the teacher, so she becomes even more familiar in coming days. On another day right before school starts, take your child for a special picnic at the school playground: having had fun there, knowing her way around the swings, will make her more comfortable on the first day.

Pretend School

Before school starts, begin the practice of "playing school" for a week, with your child's stuffed animals filling in as some of the students. Engage in some of the activities you know are standard at your child's new school, such as blocks or story hour. If you can get the names of a few other children who will be in the class, invite one or two over to join the pretend, and make sure to include a fun snack.

Drop-off Rituals

Saying good-bye is terribly hard, especially at the beginning, so think beforehand about a ritual that might ease the transition for your child. Elinor Craig found her son settled in quickly after she let him choose a secret code word on the way: when he said "it's fire engines, Mom," it meant he was ready for her to leave. One mother kisses her daughter's hand before she goes, and tells her it's a magic, all-day kiss: if she gets lonely and holds the hand to her lips, she'll get a "love buzz." Create a secret "big boy" or "big girl" handshake and hug combination, express your love in words, then if possible, get your child engaged with some toys on a table or a book on the floor before leaving. Never sneak out!

Celebrating Back-to-School Days

Even for older kids, the first day of a new school year is a big deal. Thoughtfully celebrating these days is one way to convey a sense that learning is a joy.

Think Harry Potter

Muggles don't get school supplies as nifty as pet owls and magic wands, but make your school shopping into a fun outing including lunch, and let your kids pick as many items as possible, even if their taste appalls you. Harry loves going back to Hogwarts partly because he had such memorable experiences there, so on the night before school starts, go around the table and talk about the most memorable events from the previous school year. Talk about the school play, a favorite teacher, the science experiment that blew up. The Giehl family of Colorado has a feast in the dining room on the night before, and gives each kid a school-related present, such as a fancy pencil box or a globe.

Front-Step Photos

Many parents take photos of their kids dressed up in new clothes, carrying new backpacks and lunchboxes, but posed in the same spot on the front steps. It's wonderful to look at these photos over the years, and maybe even combine them in one collage.

Bus Stop Party

Gail Spencer always starts out the year by providing juice and bagels to the 10 or so kids who wait at the bus stop with her kids.

Pep Talk in Chalk

In Maryland, Kunni Biener used to wake up extra early on the first day, so she could write messages to her daughters on the sidewalk that led to their school. They giggled as they walked along reading "Good Luck!" and "Have Fun!" and when they reached high school, they started writing messages to each other in the street on the first day.

Rewarding Good Work

Basically, I agree with Alfie Kohn, author of *Punished by Rewards*, that it's better (and more effective) to instill a love of learning than to try bribing a kid to succeed. Here are some rituals I think offer positive encouragement.

Report Card Dinners

The Suttons of Casper, Wyoming, don't eat out that often, but have a ritual of a restaurant dinner for the whole family every time report cards come out. "They mostly get straight A's, but we have the dinners no matter what," says Mary Sutton. "We feel it's important to reward the effort." Even more important, she says, she and her husband feel like they really get caught up with their kids' school lives at these relaxed meals. Thus, these dinners are more about celebrating their children as students then they are about tying certain rewards to specific achievements.

Book Rewards

Books should be treasured, and one way to reinforce that is to make books the reward for good work. When my son was learning to read, we had "reading treasure hunts," where he had to read clues all over the house. After each hunt, he put a sticker on a sheet taped to the fridge and, after 10 stickers, I took him to the bookstore and let him pick out a book.

March's
Ms. Frizzle Award
goes to
Elizabeth

Ms. Frizzle Awards

One of the problems with rewarding good grades is that it encourages kids to take easy courses and avoid challenges. My favorite teaching philosophy is that of the fictional teacher, Ms. Frizzle, from the *Magic School Bus* series on public TV. "Take chances, make mistakes, get messy!" is her motto, and such behaviors lead to learning. Every month during the school year, give the Ms. Frizzle Award (a piece of white paper with fancy writing) to the family member who follows her advice and learns the most—parents included.

Homework Rituals

If kids learn early to set aside specific times for homework, they'll develop the discipline they will need all the way through school and beyond. Establish the time for homework the first day of school, and dedicate a special "Homework Zone" in a bedroom, kitchen, or den.

Brain Food

It's good to develop a transition ritual from school to home, with a snack and some goof-off time to start. Physical activity could be included, a quick phone call to a best friend, or 15 minutes of a favorite computer game, but limit the time. Some kids like to take off their shoes or change clothes.

Q/A Partners

It can get pretty boring sitting in your room staring at a textbook. Parents can help make it more lively partly by drilling their kids on material that requires rote memorization. My friend Jean Donaldson used to toss a koosh ball back and forth with her kids while they recited math tables or spelling test words; the physical activity kept them from getting too lethargic, and I suspect the rhythm worked like a mnemonic device, helping to anchor the data in their brains.

Show and Tell

Part of the daily homework ritual should include a parental review of what's been done. Some kids feel a sense of accomplishment if they can make a checkmark on the calendar when they finish, or add a sticker. Compliment perseverance as well as creativity. You might create a winding-down ritual of a warm bath or a back rub, or end the day by reading aloud from a book your kids enjoy.

Sunday Sundaes

It's important to set specific homework rituals for the weekends as well, so everything doesn't get left till the last minute. One family gets together in the kitchen on Sunday nights for "make-your-own sundaes," but only those with finished homework can come. You might have special treat food for weekend homework sessions: instead of serving popcorn when you watch videos, save it for homework period.

More Homework Rituals

Sentenced to Laughter

It's good to develop family rituals related to learning apart from the school curriculum. By regularly including games where you play with words and use your brains for fun, you show that creative thinking is a lifelong form of play. There are plenty of great word games, including Scrabble, but it's also fun to buy a set of words to stick on your fridge. Magnetic Poetry® has an early reader version, small words in big print, and you can keep them in an empty coffee can in the kitchen. Try to get every family member to invent a sentence a day—the more absurd the better—and read them aloud at dinner.

Country of the Week

Once a week, on Sunday night or Monday morning, announce a country the family will focus on that week. Pick a country that's in the news at that time, and start by looking up its location on a map or globe. Talk about why it's newsworthy, and help the kids look up its language, history, and customs on the Internet or at the library.

Lesson of the Week

Once a week, during a family meeting or Sunday dinner, have each person in the family share something valuable or fascinating he or she learned that week. Again, you reinforce that learning is a lifelong activity. At the same time, this exercise works as a lesson review for kids, and may actually make them realize they learned something useful.

Homework Websites

www.factmonster.com has won web design awards and been cited by *Time* magazine and others as a fun, easy-to-use site packed with reference materials.

www.kidsclick.com is a mother-run source of hundreds of educational software titles, in case you home school or want to reinforce the lessons learned at school.

Playing Hooky

In general, I don't advocate teaching kids to skip school. However, I know many families who allow for one or two special days a year and their kids haven't turned into habitual truants.

A Day with Mom

Julie Stockler was allowed to play hooky one day a year when she was young, and has passed that tradition on to her daughters. When she was young, she would use her day off to go shopping with her mother at a department store and eat lunch in the ladies' tearoom. Her girls prefer to go to the movies or skiing, but treasure the one-on-one time with her as much as the forbidden pleasure of skipping out on school.

Surprise Kidnap

One mother I know surprises her kids by "kidnapping" them from school one day a year. She pays attention to when tests and school field trips are scheduled, and picks a day when they won't miss much. The kids go off to school, their mother takes a shower and dresses, then she shows up at school and surprises them. Once they get in the car, the lucky kid gets to decide how to spend the day.

Museum Days

If you've ever been to a major museum like the Natural History Museum in New York City, which has one of the greatest dinosaur collections anywhere, you know how crowded it gets on weekends and school holidays. I want to start an annual ritual where my son and I skip school and work to see the T-Rex up-close and personal. He loves the dino-shaped chicken nuggets in the museum cafeteria, but an outing like this feeds the mind more than the belly.

Sty Day

A friend of mine used to take one mental health day a year with her daughter, when they would never get out of their pajamas. They watched television and ate junk food all day. No one would argue this is educational, but it sure was a fun contrast to work and school, and it didn't hurt the daughter, who later graduated from one of the country's top law schools.

End-of-School-Year Rituals

Teacher Tribute

To encourage gratitude and practice writing, have your children write and decorate thank-you notes to their teachers. Encourage them to list specific areas in which they learned a lot, or an area where the teacher provided crucial, extra assistance. They might also bring a small gift, such as flowers.

Kid's Choice Dinner

Food isn't the only thing kids choose when the Fitch family of Columbus, Ohio, celebrates the last day of school. They not only pick the menu, but also where and when to eat it. When Corey Fitch was nine, the year the ritual began, he decided he wanted to eat carryout Chinese food on the steps of his elementary school—at midnight. "We sat there eating noodles and talking about the past year," says Sally Fitch. "It was wild and crazy, and he loved it."

Library Payback

Patrice Kyger always takes her kids out to dinner on the last day, to their favorite restaurant. When they graduate from elementary school, they are allowed to pick out a book and have her buy it for the school library, an act which makes them feel very grown-up.

Welcome Summer Party

Carolyn Hecht's son, now grown, always celebrated the last day of school by hosting a huge watermelon fight in the backyard. "There were always seven or eight boys, and it was a big, messy fight that lasted all afternoon," says Carolyn. There are other activities and foods for welcoming summer in the backyard: you can serve lemonade or ice cream cones, and if it's sunny, start the summer off with a squirt gun and water-balloon battle.

How to Make an End-of-Year Award Poster

Materials

Sturdy poster board from office supply or crafts store; markers; ribbon; scissors; class photo of the child that year or a photocopy of same; pictures of your child at school (if you have them); magazine photos.

Instructions

Cut the school photo into a round or oval shape, and glue it into the center of the poster. Color around the photograph, making an elaborate border. Write across the top in marker: "Star Student (child's name)" and the year. In an oval pattern around the central photo, place photos either of your child doing different activities, such as sports or studying, or drawings of such, or magazine photos that suggest these things. Write underneath each image something your child did or learned. Glue one end of a piece of ribbon next to the central photo, and glue the other end near the image of an accomplishment. Repeat the process, attaching additional ribbons to the central photograph and the surrounding images, so the ribbons radiate out like spokes of a wheel. Have a special end of school family dinner like the Giehls of Colorado, and present the poster at dinner.

Summer Vacation Rituals

A balance needs to be found between the overprogrammed school year life of many kids, and a summer of free-form loafing. Family rituals for this time of year often center on summer food, trips to the local pool, and backyard games. Some fun ideas to try:

Books and Cones

One reason my son reads so much in the summer is that the local library gives the kids a "summer passport" to list all the books they read (or have read to them). Any child who clocks 12 hours of reading in a summer gets a free sundae at the local ice cream store in the fall. Why not make books a sweet treat now: go to the library every two weeks, and stop for an ice cream cone after every visit.

New and Barbecued

Once a week, have a simple backyard barbecue, but invite a family in the neighborhood or from your children's school that hasn't been to your home before. Make a pact with your kids that you'll serve some of their favorite foods like hot dogs and chips, but try one new grilled item each time, like grilled peppers, corn on the cob, or chicken-and-mushroom kabobs.

Tour Your Town

One summer weekend each year, pretend your family just arrived as tourists, and see the best your town has to offer. Visit historical sites, eat in the cool new restaurant, take a long bike ride through neighborhoods you've never visited. Take photos in front of landmarks, buy t-shirts, and send postcards.

Make a Movie

After school ends, have a "story conference" and come up with a wacky plot in which every family member plays at least one character. Design costumes. Over the course of the summer, shoot one scene at a time, in different locations. For credits, film one of your kids typing the title and list of actors on a computer screen. At summer's end, invite friends and family to the "premiere." Next summer: shoot a sequel, or the prequel.

Getting There:
Rituals for Cars and Planes

Vacation spots are mostly heavenly, but getting there can be challenging. Many families have created rituals that make the journey actually feel like part of the vacation.

Fuss Towns

Polly Mead drastically reduced the number of car fights between her four kids by creating the ritual of "fuss towns." Before a long drive, she locates a town roughly halfway to the day's destination. The kids aren't allowed to fuss and yell until they get to the outskirts of the designated fuss town, and then those behaviors are mandatory. They erupt and explode with a vengeance, but once they reach the other end of town, they calm back down. Mostly.

Storyteller for Hire

Some parents keep their kids occupied watching movies on a car-adapted television and VCR, but I'd argue for a story the whole family can share. We always take chapter books on car trips, but the designated reader gets pooped before long. A great ritual is to get an unabridged book-on-tape (or compact disc) from the local library. The story becomes a memorable part of your summer. Ask the librarian for age-appropriate books, but our favorites are the Harry Potter books; *Trumpet of the Swan* read by author E.B. White; and *The Indian in the Cupboard* read by author Lynne Reid Banks.

Rhyme Games

Car games are essential, and many of the best don't even require props. Have one of the parents start a nonsense sentence, which every person in the car has to rhyme with another sentence. Nancy Shaw used to play a game like this with her children in the car, and later turned it into a series of best-selling picture books with names like *Sheep on a Jeep* and *Sheep on a Ship*.

Games Website

www.liveandlearn.com/cargame.html is a site that sells educational games. But this site also includes the rules for such classic car games as 20 Questions.

Being There:
Rituals for Peak Vacations

Porcupine Award

The Routh family of Iowa spotted a live porcupine while hiking in the Rocky Mountains and declared it the strangest-looking creature they had ever seen outside a zoo. Thus was born the Porcupine Award, given to the family member who spots the weirdest animal on any trip, or even a long family hike. Mary Routh says it's great because even the baby of the family sometimes wins. There isn't an actual certificate given by the Rouths, but your family could create one. Or buy a cheap trophy and pass it from room to room back home, as different people "win."

Every Picture Tells a Story

Think ahead about a loose plot that could be tied to your destination, and take a series of fun photos to tell that story. It could be as simple as creating a scrapbook travelogue starring your toddler daughter's frayed teddy bear. Photograph him at the pool (not too close to the water), asleep in her bed, viewing the local sights. Onc family I know has a goofy Christmas gift exchange in which the same wacky object is passed from household to household: whoever gets the thing in a given year invariably takes it on vacation and photographs the thing somewhere scenic.

Arriving in Style

Some families vacation at the same cabin, resort, or campground every year, and love to settle in with a ritual that makes them feel at home and ready to relax. They might head to a nearby stream, take off their shoes and go wading, or stop by the same fried-clam stand for their favorite vacation chow. When we visit my husband's cousin on a lake in New Hampshire every August, we always watch the sun set while sitting on the dock and sipping a special lemon drink. But you can also start an arrival ritual that works wherever you go. If you arrive after dark, for example, you can give the kids glowing fluorescent sticks and let them run wildly in circles around your cottage or campsite.

Family Reunions

A regular reunion, even a small one, helps kids grow up with a sense of family history and a feeling of belonging. Living so far from each other, such gifts are even more valuable. Here are some fun reunion ideas shared by families:

Big Event

The Love family reunion, begun in 1976 as a weekend get-together, now attracts 300 family members and lasts four days. The semiannual reunions always include a golf tournament and talent night, but a special feature is the family mentoring program. Every child between 7 and 15 is paired with a family mentor. Even between reunions, the children check in with their mentors about their career aspirations, listing five steps they'll take to achieve them.

One Generation Is Enough

Every year, Amy Cordell has a weekend reunion with her five sisters (and one brother), and they call it the Sisters Convention. They meet at a hotel or one of the sibling's homes and the main activity is talk. "Because the gap between youngest and oldest is 12 years, this has finally made it possible for us to really know each other," says Amy. They have been known to make reunion t-shirts, but usually each one brings a favorite book or product (hair mousse, once) to share with the others.

Family Farm

Seidemanns come from 24 states on the third Sunday of July for a one-day reunion of this clan at the patriarch's Wisconsin farm. The descendants of German immigrants always have a kuchen (coffee cake) contest, and the entries are auctioned off to help pay for the reunion. Annual features include food, games, and a talent show, and the barn is full of family furniture and artifacts from eight generations.

Tip: If you have a big reunion and reserve a sizable block of rooms, many hotels will throw in a free room or hospitality suite.

More Reunion Ideas

Family Alphabet Chant

Create a family cheer or song in which each letter of the family's name stands for something. Try to weave family history into it, letting the letters stand for a special hometown, professions of prominent family members, or family lore such as war heroism. Repeat it at every reunion.

Family Olympics

The Bode family picks a special theme for each reunion. The Olympics was one of the most popular, kicking off with a parade in which each family represented a different country. The games were things like "chugging contests" with Dixie cups full of root beer, and the day ended with an international buffet (Swedish meatballs, German potato salad, etc.) and a medals ceremony.

Cousins Camp

One form of reunion is when Grandma invites all the grandchildren to visit her at the same time, for a weekend or longer. Since she misses many of her grandkids' birthdays throughout the year, every summer Patty Mac Hewitt celebrates "Everybody's Birthday" at her summer house on a lake in New Hampshire. There is plenty of cake and ice cream for all the kids, and everybody gets a present: usually a toy good for either sex which can be left at Grandma's till next year.

Five tips from *Reunions* magazine

1. Give yourself far more lead time than you expect you'll need.

2. Never do it alone: create a committee of family members to help with every phase.

3. Make it affordable for everyone.

4. Provide activities for all, especially kids who tend to get bored quickly.

5. Explore family history: tell stories, organize displays, visit cemeteries.

Reunions is published six times a year (800-373-7933) and also has an excellent website, **www.reunionsmag.com**.

Still More Reunion Ideas

Reunion Quilt

The Gines family takes turn hosting their reunion, and each year the host family passes out fabric already cut into 6-inch squares. Each family unit attending decorates their fabric (with fabric paint if they don't sew), and the seamstresses in the clan stage a sort of quilting bee during the get-together. The finished quilt is given to the family that hosted that year.

Family Cookbook

Many families who hold reunions regularly sell items like coffee mugs and t-shirts. If it's a big reunion, this can be a good moneymaker, and even if it's a smaller group, at least everyone gets a neat souvenir and there is some money for postage and other reunion expenses. A number of families sell reunion cookbooks, thick with favorite family recipes. With reunions that attract 300 or more guests, this too can help raise funds. But it doesn't have to be ambitious: ask every family coming to your next reunion to bring 5 or 10 favorite recipes, and publish the resulting "cookbook" on your home computer in time for Christmas.

Memorial Service

Many families like to include a memorial service, to honor both departed individuals and the family's collective history. The Bullock family reunion, inspired in part by Alex Haley's book *Roots*, features an especially dramatic candle-lighting ritual during its Saturday night banquet. The lights are turned low, gospel music plays in the background, and candles are lit: a thick white one for the patriarch, George Bullock, Sr., and smaller white ones for his departed children.

More Reunion Resources

Two popular and useful books are *Family Reunions* by Jennifer Crichton and *Your Family Reunion: How to Plan It, Organize It, and Enjoy It* by George G. Morgan.

There are many websites, but **Family-Reunion.com** (don't forget the hyphen) has won awards. It includes a reunion planner, links to many other websites, and an extensive list of hotels and resorts that cater to reunions.

Rare and Made-Up Family Holidays

It's a wonderful moment when a child realizes that nobody else on the planet celebrates the same wacky holiday that his or her family invented.

Crazy Food Day

The Taylor family of Stratford, Connecticut, started this tradition one year during Christmas vacation: on Crazy Food Day, all the meals are mixed up. They might eat lunch or dinner for breakfast, and breakfast for lunch. This day usually gets chosen when school is closed due to snow, or there's a vacation day with no events planned. Everybody stays in his or her pajamas all day.

Kids' Day

Some kids have lobbied their parents for a children's equivalent of Mother's Day and Father's Day. The Hains girls of Maryland get to pick a special family activity, and each gets a small gift. Patrice Kyger takes it a step further: Son's Day is the second Sunday in July, and Daughter's Day comes on the second Sunday in August. A special outing like a picnic or miniature golf is planned, and the siblings talk about what's good about having a sister or brother, depending on the day.

Family Happiness Party

In Merchantville, New Jersey, Susan Lynch and her daughters know just what to do on days when everyone in the family is down in the dumps. They declare a Family Happiness Party, and get ready to cheer themselves up with such treats as make-your-own sundaes.

Yes Day

Darcie Gore wrote in *Family Fun* magazine that she got tired of saying "no" to her three girls constantly, and decided to declare the next Saturday "Yes Day." She started a "Yes Jar," where her daughters write down things they can't do immediately, such as "wear my Cinderella dress all day." On Yes Day each month, the activity requests are read, and then acted on. The first Yes Day began with a breakfast of chocolate milk and donuts, and included such activities as freeze tag, a pillow fight, and the application of toenail polish.

More Invent-a-Holiday Ideas

Ground Hog Day

This holiday isn't invented, but who do you know who actually celebrates it? Nancy Dodge, the mother of five in Princeton, New Jersey, says her family really needs a holiday around February 2 "when the winter is looking endless and bleak." Basically, the Dodge family eats a lot of junk food on Ground Hog Day and watches back-to-back movies, mostly on a baseball theme, though they've been known to watch the movie named for the holiday.

Mess Day

The idea is to take all the ordinary household rules, and for one entire day, turn them upside down. Let everybody wear their grubbiest clothes, and never comb their hair. Table manners aren't allowed, and all meals should be eaten on a picnic blanket on the floor, preferably while watching television. Toys are never to be put away so that playing never has to stop.

Overcoat Day

In New York City, Mary Beaton and Jels McCaulay celebrate this holiday with their two daughters. On the first really cold day of the year, they call friends and family and proclaim "Overcoat Day." Depending on whether it's a weekend or weekday, up to 30 people show up in mittens, scarves and warm coats and crowd onto the family's outdoor deck. The adults drink champagne, while the kids clink sippy cups of juice together. "Wintery" books like *The Snowy Day* by Ezra Jack Keats are read aloud, and the kids make snowman decorations out of cottonballs and construction paper.

Alice in Wonderland Day

Declare a fantasy day, and let everyone pick themes, food, and activities. Go to a special place where you'll feel really huge or really tiny, like Alice after she eats the magic food. Have a Mad Hatter's Tea Party. Read or talk about your favorite fantasy books, such as Harry Potter. Mix magic potions. Learn magic tricks.

Daily, Weekly, and Monthly Rituals

Daily Rituals

Mealtimes
Grace

Even for families who aren't religious, saying grace before a meal can be a wonderful ritual of transition. It functions like a call to reconnection after a day of separation.

Simple and Good

Some of the most profound graces are the simplest, such as the lovely Quaker grace "Us and this: God bless." I also like "Now my plate is full, but soon it will be gone. Thank you for my food, and please help those with none."

Sing for Your Supper

The Hodge family sings together often, including for grace. A favorite is the Johnny Appleseed song which goes: "Oh the Lord is good to me, and so I thank the Lord/For giving me the things I need/The sun and the rain and the appleseed/The Lord is good to me."

Silent Prayers

Elizabeth Fergus-Jean prefers that her husband and children observe a moment of simple silence before eating. "I've told my kids that this should be a moment of thanks, but also a moment of connectedness."

Holding Hands

The Michaels of Minneapolis say a simple grace, and then all squeeze hands before they eat.

Taking Turns

The Mowbray family takes turns saying grace. Often they improvise, but in a pinch they keep returning to a traditional Catholic blessing, "Bless us, O Lord, and these thy gifts, which we are about to receive from your bounty. Through Christ our Lord, Amen."

Choosing a Grace

Two terrific books are *A Grateful Heart: Daily Blessings for the Evening Meal from Buddha to the Beatles* edited by M.J. Ryan, and *The Classic Treasury of Children's Prayers* compiled by Susan Cuthbert, which also includes bedtime prayers, and more.

Unconventional Meals

Don't be afraid to break some rules about family dinners if it works for your family. Tailor meal traditions to your schedules, passions, and personalities. Paper plates are fine; distractions like television aren't, as a rule.

Reading Meals

Food writer Ann Hodgman declares every other night a "reading dinner" at her house. She and her husband and their two kids can either read or draw during those meals, and books and art supplies are kept by the table in a wicker basket. Alternate nights are designated "talking dinners" and then the object is for each person to be as amusing as possible.

Finger Food Only

Once a week, serve a meal that requires absolutely no utensils and let the kids eat with their hands. Even salad and vegetables taste better that way. This could be an all-appetizer meal (be sure to include veggies and dip as one way to keep it nutritious), or an ethnic dinner like Chinese dumplings and ribs. (Don't let this coincide with a reading meal, or your books will be covered with grease!)

Indoor Picnics

Moving the meal from the table to the floor can make the same old carryout Chinese food or pizza feel like a special treat. If you don't have a picnic blanket, an old sheet works just fine and goes right into the wash afterward.

Opera Meals

One family I know occasionally declares an "opera meal," and everybody sings instead of speaking, even to ask "please, pass the butter." Being in tune isn't a requirement, and they all get pretty silly. An alternative is to try a silent meal, and see if everyone can communicate entirely with hand signals.

For more tips on memorable meals, read *Come to the Table: a Celebration of Family Life* by Doris Christopher.

Making It Special

Spotlight Dinners

Sydney Gines has these surprise dinners once or twice a year for each of her four kids. Some dinners celebrate an accomplishment such as "learning a complicated piano piece or breaking a bad habit," while others are scheduled for "a self-esteem boost." Sydney pretends company is coming, so the kids dress up a bit and expect a special dinner. When the kids come to the table, Sydney and her husband announce that the "special guest" is one of the children, and throw confetti at him or her. A small gift is given, and the whole family lauds the spotlighted child.

Soup Nights

Children's book author Martha Freeman and her family host Soup Night every Thursday from October through March. Every September, Martha sends out a standing invitation to about 60 people, friends and neighbors, to come any Thursday they want after 5:30 p.m. Many bring bread, wine, or cookies. Martha makes huge pots of soup, and provides paper bowls and spoons, plus apple juice for the kids. Her three children love the casual party atmosphere and seeing all their friends.

Sunday Kids' Choice

Teacher Anne Hodge wanted her kids to share the kitchen chores and make Sunday dinners special. She started Kids' Choice, and though her three children have to take turns cooking and cleaning up on that night, they also take turns making up funny rules for the meal. On Lego Night, the table was decorated with Legos, and then there was "Changing Seats Night," and the time they could eat only with spoons.

Toast Night

Barb Brock, a professor in Spokane, decided to make one dinner a week special, so on Thursdays, the family uses their fancy dishes even for carryout. Also, on that night, each member of the family makes a toast. Making a toast is something kids love, as it seems like such a grown-up gesture. Eating by candlelight once a week is also a treat for kids.

Conversation Rituals

With a little planning and prodding, even hungry, preoccupied kids can make sparkling conversation.

Current Events

Gloria Uhler's kids had to come to the dinner table nightly with one topic of conversation related to current events. The rule was that each child introduced his or her subject and shared some information they had heard or read. Everyone else in the family had to ask at least one question to keep the conversation going. This could be a weekly tradition for some.

Family News

Patrice Kyger insists that her children each share a "new and good" that happened to them during the day. Complaints and bad news are allowed, but never without the compensating good news. The family is also on the lookout for what they call "blurbs," random comments that strike everyone but the speaker as out-of-context and hilarious; these are written down in a special book.

Conversation-in-a-Jar

One way to get the conversation rolling is to keep a jar in the middle of the table full of offbeat topics. Get a ceramic pot or empty tin and fill it with a couple dozen strips of colored paper marked with the sort of questions celebrities get asked. At meals, each family member picks one. Some ideas: "The most surprising thing about me is . . . " "Three things that make me happy are . . . " "The world would be a better place if . . ." "The best book I read recently was . . ." and "If I had a million dollars . . . " Allow time for each topic to be fully discussed before pulling out another question. You can recycle the topics, and keep adding new ones.

Bedtime

This is a great time to gently reconnect with your kids and prepare them for fear-free dreaming. Having a soothing, cuddly go-to-sleep ritual every night, preferably at close to the same time, vastly reduces bedtime battles.

Planting Good Dreams

Some parents draw a circle on their child's forehead at bedtime "to put the good dreams in," but Sue McCandless goes even further. At two, Sue's daughter started having terrifying nightmares, and Sue started inventing good dreams at bedtime to drive them away. The suggested dreams are vivid and action-packed. "I'll say, 'Dream you're riding a two-wheeler without training wheels in a race and your helmet is pink,'" says Sue. The outcome of the dream is left for Taylor to finish in her sleep. The girl says she often dreams what her mother suggests.

Proud-Prouds

Tim Mullin wanted to end his daughters' days on a positive note and started the ritual of asking them at bedtime to share something they did that day of which they are proud. Then, he and his wife add something else the girls did that the parents want to specially praise. Tim and his wife often learn things during Proud-Prouds they didn't know about their kids' day at school, and they try to praise things that reflect their values. "We tell them we're proud by how hard they tried something and not just the successes," says Tricia. "I don't want them to think perfection is the goal."

Monster Spray

Matthew Pompi invented monster spray when his son complained there were monsters in his bedroom at night. Matthew simply filled a plastic plant-spritzer bottle with water and pasted a colorful label to the front. At bedtime, father and son spray under the bed, in the closet, and anywhere else monsters might lurk. Nathan takes the bottle to the bathroom during the night and for overnights at Grandma's.

More Bedtime Rituals

Touch the Darkness

Some children respond well to rituals that ease them toward bedtime one step at a time. Allison Defferner does a ritual with her infant daughter that her own mother began: they open the front door and literally reach out their palms to "touch" the night before bedtime. Kathy Schuessler always drops her kids off in their rooms by linking them all together in a train-like file and "choo-chooing" down the hall.

Good-Night Family Tree

When my son was an infant, I started a bedtime ritual that includes good-nights "to all the people Max loves." The circle of family and friends that are named has changed as he ages, with friends and teachers included now. I go through all the aunts and uncles and cousins and babysitters, and we always end with "good night to all the grandparents in Heaven. Good night to ALL the people we love." My son falls asleep feeling surrounded by love, and it's a great way to remind him of relatives he rarely gets to see.

Bedtime Stories

Telling stories is a great tradition in many families and cultures, and one of the advantages over stories in books is that you can tell them in the dark. Kyna Tabor tells elaborate bedtime stories about her family's pet cats, "an ever-growing cat nation." Kyna finds her kids hurry to get into their pajamas and brush their teeth at night, because they can't wait to hear the day's installment about "our cat who was a princess in another land." I used to tell stories about an invented polar bear named Pete, and my husband specialized in the adventures of Jake, a blue bulldozer.

Tip: If you have bedtime stories you tell again and again, whether classic fairy tales or your own inventions, it's a great idea to tape record a few. The tapes will come in handy when you've got a sore throat or have to go on out-of-town business trips.

Even More Bedtime Rituals (because they're so important)

Map Ritual

One father I know uses bedtime to teach geography. His son has an enormous world map on the wall of his bedroom, and at bedtime, he closes his eyes and points somewhere on it. He and his father sit quietly and talk about what it's like in that place: language, history, climate, and customs. At times, they get so intrigued they look up additional info the next day.

Bedtime Countdown

To keep her kids from popping out of bed constantly because they forgot to brush their teeth or collect their stuffed animals, Cora Berry created a bedtime checklist that stays on the bedroom door. As they go through each item on the list, which includes a prayer and bedtime story, she calls out "check." After the last item, the lights are turned off.

In-Bed Massage

Comforting physical touch is a great way to relax and let go of the day. Some parents have a tradition of rubbing their children's backs or necks at bedtime, and find being relaxed sometimes helps normally reticent children share confidences. Others massage their children's feet (warning: if they are especially ticklish, this might unrelax them). Scalp massage can also be extremely soothing, and some girls love to have their hair brushed and smoothed last thing.

Beyond the Bedroom Wall

Novelist Larry Woiwode wrote a luminous novel by this name, and the title refers to a child's bedtime ritual. The boy would lie in bed and picture himself in the room, then roam in his mind past the walls to his street, then to the edge of his town, and on and on. It's a wonderful meditative exercise, like stretching one's mind out to infinity.

Blow Out the Light

Turning off the light can be a tough transition for small ones. Coming up with a ritual where they "help blow out the light" and make a wish may help. Or let them tuck in favorite dolls or stuffed animals.

Bedtime Reading Rituals

For some busy parents, bedtime is the only time they get to read aloud to their kids and they want to make the most of it. For children, the combination of snuggling and story is heaven on earth. To avoid whining, some parents set limits, such as three picture books for a toddler, or just one chapter a night.

Six tips for starting a bedtime reading ritual:

1. Pick books at or below your child's current level, as they may be tired and able to take in less at this hour.

2. Start bedtime reading in infancy, and not just with cloth or board books. Simple picture books or rhyming books are great.

3. Steer away from anything scary; even at seven, many fantasy books, including Harry Potter, gave my son scary dreams.

4. It's generally best to read in the same place each night, whether it's a comfy sofa in the den, your child's bed, or your own. The books will vary widely, but as in any ritual, it's more reassuring if some parts of the ritual stay the same.

5. Always say the name of the author and illustrator aloud along with the title, as this helps kids understand that books are created by people. They will soon spot similarities between an author's works, like those of Dr. Seuss.

6. Don't stop when your child learns to read. Share the reading, perhaps taking turns reading a page at a time.

Choosing Books

The whimsical Chinaberry catalog picks great books by age group and provides tips for reading to very young kids. Call 800-776-2242 for the free catalog, or go to **www.chinaberry.com**.

In *The Read-Aloud Handbook*, Jim Trelease explains why reading to kids matters so much, but also includes detailed lists of books for every age. His excellent website is **www.trelease-on-reading.com**.

My own favorites for toddlers and preschoolers: *The Velveteen Rabbit* and anything by Bill Peet.

Bedtime Prayers

The idea that someone powerful is watching over them while they sleep (in addition to their sometimes fallible parents) is enormously comforting to children. Bedtime prayers are also a wonderful way to pass on religious traditions and beliefs, and help teach a child empathy and gratitude.

God Bless

One of the simplest and most enduring bedtime prayers is for the child to ask God to bless each and every person important to him or her.

Thankfulness

Even before we attended church together, I started saying a prayer in bed with my son every night. It's sort of a loose conversation with God, asking for help and guidance for our family and others, but the heart of it is gratitude. I always start by saying, "Thank you for this day, God," no matter how rocky it's been, and end with, "Thank you for all the good things in our lives," some of which I list.

At first my son was mystified that I seemed to speak to the ceiling, but now he often inserts his own pleas and thanks to God.

Widen the Circle

Author Esther Ilnisky suggests that parents get their children to pray for others using what she calls "identity prayers." They can pray for all the kids in the world who share their name, or are the same age. She also suggests that if a child is having problems at school, they pray for God to help them, plus the other kids at the school having a hard time. Ilnisky wrote *Let the Children Pray*, an excerpt of which can be found at **www.christianitytoday.com**.

Prayer Search

Any house of worship can provide guidance in finding suitable religious prayers for bedtime. At multidenominational websites like **www.beliefnet.com**, you can ask religious experts and other parents what prayers they like.

Hello and Good-bye Rituals

Even a quick good-bye ritual makes parting easier. As kids get older and more independent, they still rely on the kisses you blow to them as the bus drives off. It's also good to create rituals that lovingly reunite our families.

Special Handshakes

On a recent Oprah Winfrey show, a father demonstrated the complicated handshakes he does with his son and daughter as part of a morning good-bye ritual. These were more like elaborate hand ballets than handshakes, but performing them before separating gives the kids a vivid reminder that their connection to Dad is close, and unique.

Homecoming Blessing

To really feel conscious of resuming the family connection, some people devise simple rituals of homecoming at day's end. Kathleen O'Connell Chesto, a writer on Catholic family ritual, suggests hugging the kids when they return from school, and saying this simple prayer: "Lord, help us to be present to you in one another. Amen."

Circle Hugs

One family I know takes a moment each morning before they all head off to work and school to do a quick circle hug in the kitchen. They face the center, bow their heads, and ask God to "bless this day and our love for each other."

Daily Wishes

Along with good-bye morning hugs in our house, we try to say at least two things we hope for the person that day. My son might say to his father, "For today, I hope your commute is easy and your work is fun." Tailoring the wishes to the day proves we're paying attention to each other's lives, a comforting proof of love.

Stuffed Animals in the Trees

Right before meeting my son's bus, I grab a handful of his favorite stuffed animals, and perch them on tree branches, rocks, and the swing set. He races off the bus to find them and always walks in the front door grinning.

Rituals to Keep the Peace

Kids will bicker and fight, especially siblings. But sometimes, a brief ritual can calm the combatants. Teaching young kids to avoid violence is a powerful life lesson.

Family Huddle

When the two Abbe kids have been fighting, especially in the car, their mother hollers out "family huddle time." Even in a parking lot, they stop and huddle like teammates, stack their hands up in the center of the circle, yell out the family cheer ("Let's go, Abbes!"), and punch their fists to the sky. Afterward, they go on their way as a united force.

Crazy Dance Party

The Pfeiffer family says family unity is always restored if they can laugh together, so when any of them feels it's needed, he or she calls out "Crazy Dance Party" and starts a countdown from 10 to 1. By 1, someone has found a rock oldies radio station to listen to, and they dance like lunatics till everybody is laughing.

Three tips on handling anger from expert Naomi Drew

1. Create a cooling-off ritual for yourself: breathe deeply three times, then get a drink of water, go into another room and listen to quiet music, or light a candle and calm your thoughts.

2. Help your children to create their own cooling-off rituals. Some kids pet their dog, run around the yard, wash their face, write in a journal, or take their frustration out by making something out of clay.

3. Peace shield ritual: put a drop or two of essential oil of lavender in a spray bottle full of water. During a calm moment, have your children close their eyes and imagine a shield of light, protecting them from hurt and anger. Spray some lavender water in their direction to "lock in" the shield's power. Next time they get upset, have them imagine the peace shield protecting them from hurt and anger.

Naomi Drew's latest book is *Hope and Healing: Peaceful Parenting in an Uncertain World*. Write to **win47win@aol.com** for her free e-mail newsletter, Peaceful Parenting.

Chore Rituals

Mary Poppins was right about that spoonful of sugar; we all have duties and chores, but rituals can liven them up. That applies to chores we assign our kids, and chores we must do ourselves, when they'd rather we play. If all else fails, invent specific silly songs for different chores; this works well with toddlers. Whistle while you work!

Laundry

One of our babysitters started this ritual of letting my son "ride" the bulging laundry bag as it's pulled across the floor to the laundry room, and now I perform it weekly. "Oh my goodness, my laundry is heavy!" I'll moan as I tug him along. Then, I'll pretend I'm going to throw my son in the washer, and set him down on top of it. One mother I know does laundry with her daughters on Friday night, creating "intermissions" in their video-watching to go change loads. The girls bring their own dirty clothes to the washer in a baby carriage.

Grocery Shopping

Little kids can become very cranky sitting in those cramped metal carts. In addition to bringing a snack like a baggy full of Goldfish® crackers, I always told my son stories when we went on errands. My invented polar bear, Pete, would be in the grocery store with us getting into trouble, usually by climbing into the freezers and eating all the Klondike bars. We had brief but fun rituals for different sections of the market: when we came to the seafood section, Max always said "hello" to the live lobsters in the tank.

Yardwork

You'll get a lot more work done if your kids can help, or feel like they have. Get duplicates of some of your tools, especially gloves and hoes, and give them their own part of the yard to tend. Have a regular routine such as always checking under certain rocks to look for insects, always climbing a certain tree, always leaving seeds or breadcrumbs in the backyard for the birds.

Pet Rituals

I know a guy who sends postcards to his parrot when he goes on vacation, and Halloween costumes for pets are a booming business. Many of the rituals we enact with our pets are more for ourselves, but routine comforts animals of all kinds. And rituals can help young kids relish the regular duties of pet ownership.

Walking the Dog

Dogs demand ritual and respond to it as devotedly as children, and this is especially true with the all-important routine of daily walks. Dog owners tend to have prewalk rituals that include verbal cues and flourishes such as having the dog carry his leash to the door. Adding on silly songs or other fun antics makes this more enjoyable for kids, too. Whenever my son visits Auntie Na (aka my husband's ex-wife Anita), he loves to walk her dog, Lily, and always starts with a special song ("Gather the poop papers, Peggy, we're going for a walk . . .").

Mealtimes

Never tease a hungry dog about food, but many owners like to have their dog sit first and give him or her a pat on the head before placing the bowl on the floor. If your child wants to sing a special song or even say grace before the cat gets supper, why not? It will help a kid remember to feed his or her pet because the routine is spiced with fun.

Birthdays

The Pompi family celebrates the birthdays of all seven of their cats, and their dog. The cats get a can of tuna decorated with a candle stuck in it, and the dog gets a meaty bone from the butcher with a candle. The dog gets the biggest party, because he's the oldest. Naturally, the Pompis sing "Happy Birthday" before helping their pets blow out candles.

Baths

For most dogs, a bath is not a treat. Try to make it fun by having the kids put on their bathing suits and climb right into the bathtub with the dog. Pretend that you're preparing the dog for a big dog show, while drying and combing your pet, adding embellishments like ribbons and maybe taking silly photographs.

Pet Funerals

The death of a pet is a big hurt for a young child. Ritualizing that death helps the child work through a painful loss and teaches them to value all living things.

Goldfish Burial

In the book *How to Bury a Goldfish and 113 Other Family Rituals for Everyday Life*, Virginia Lang recalls the time she almost flushed her two-year-old daughter's dead fish down the toilet. Instead, she and her daughter dug a little hole together in the backyard, put the fish in the hole, and planted a flower on the spot. Her daughter invented a song about her pet. Ms. Lang recommends marking the calendar on the day a pet dies, as well as marking the ground where the pet is buried, either with a painted rock or by planting something.

Rats and Gerbils, Too

My friend Sandy Graham has found her kids grieve greatly even when a pet rat dies. Her son and daughter make a gravestone with a piece of flagstone or brick and a permanent marker. The pet is put in a metal cookie tin, resting on a scrap of fabric that is soft and pretty (often satin or velvet). They are buried by a special tree, a big cottonwood, and all four family members reminisce about the pet's exploits and character. Sandy says a prayer asking God to welcome the critter into pet heaven with all the family's previous pets.

Pet Cemetery

If yours is a critter-loving family, chances are pet funerals will become a more regular ritual than you bargained for, and you may want to create a special garden for this purpose. You might consider planting specific plants for different animals, such as catnip for your favorite cats, or bright yellow sunflowers for a pet with a sunny disposition. You can paint a special marker for each animal, or place special garden decorations here such as wind chimes or a birdbath. Inside the house, you could designate a certain wall for pet photos, or make a memorial photo album.

Sports Rituals

Most kids today participate in sports, and most families actively cheer on their favorite pro teams. Rituals can celebrate victory, ease defeat, and help us perform at our peak.

Divine Guidance

Many great athletes ask for God's help before beginning a game or contest. Kathy Chesto, the Catholic writer, always said this prayer with her track star son before he started a meet: "Those who wait for the Lord shall renew their strength/They shall mount up with wings like eagles/They shall run and not be weary/They shall walk and not be faint."

Celebrate Wins and Losses

I heard about a Little League coach who brought helium balloons to each game. The kids would release them to the skies if they won, and puncture them with a pin if they lost. Some prefer to celebrate a game well played, regardless of the outcome. My family are fanatical Cleveland Browns fans, and we always eat sundaes after watching a game on TV, either to celebrate or to console ourselves. (To help them win, we always wear team gear when we watch, hold hands during crunch plays, and tear apart our Ref doll, whose arms are attached with Velcro, during bad calls.)

Team Colors

To cheer on any team, hang crepe paper around your kitchen in the team colors and try to serve food in those colors. Milk and mashed potatoes are among the foods easily dyed with food coloring. Or, make big sugar cookies and ice them in two different colors, one on each half of the circle. Make small paper flags in team colors, glue them to toothpicks, and stick them in various foods or table decorations.

Personal Best Award

Store a few sports tokens like key chains, mini-trophies or posters to give to your child after he works especially hard in a game. Maybe she didn't score the winning goal, but made a breakthrough in catching a tough pass; show her you noticed.

Weekly Rituals

Having a weekly ritual is like a family-time insurance policy: the payoffs are definitely worth the time invested.

Dates with Dad

When people say they despair of staying close to a teenager, I tell them about Jim McCandless. Jim worked 70-hour weeks and felt he was growing distant from his son, just starting junior high. They started weekly outings, and Jim moves mountains to keep that special night open. The key: his son dictates the activity each week, whether it's playing catch, bowling, or visiting the local hobby store. Father and son were amazed at how much better they got to know, and enjoy, each other by keeping this weekly date.

Weekend Campout

Teresa Schultz-Jones lets her three kids "camp" in the family room on one weekend night, but only "if they behaved well the previous week and did their chores." The kids sleep in sleeping bags, watch videos, stay up late, and sometimes get pizza.

Kids Cook Night

When Suzy Kellett's quadruplets got old enough, she gave each one a cookbook, and scheduled them to take turns cooking dinner on Sundays. The rules are: "you must cook something you've never cooked before, and you must invite at least one guest." Her kids love it.

Surprise Excursions

Many families reserve Saturdays for errands, athletic practices, and household chores, and try to set Sunday aside as a special family day. One family I know goes to church in the morning, then saves Sunday afternoon for a special family excursion. The mother and father take turns picking the outing, keeping it secret until the last minute. One Sunday they'll go apple-picking at a local orchard, and the next week, it will be a visit to a museum or historical site. When the kids are a bit older, they will take turns picking, too.

Walking Talks

Every Sunday, take a one-hour walk in a beautiful park or nature preserve. Take turns picking a conversational topic that everyone in the family can enjoy. You might answer a question like: "If you had a time machine, where would you travel?" or, you can take the plot of a popular movie like *Toy Story* and jointly spin a yarn about your own toys in an adventure they would have while you sleep or go on vacation.

Weekly Family Nights

There are many ways to organize a weekly family night, including around religious traditions. Having even one hour to share, learn, and play together will do a lot to keep you close.

Prayer and More

The Suks of Evanston have family nights every Thursday, and they start with a kid-friendly dinner, "something like tacos that everybody loves," says L'Tishia Suk. The meal is started with a hymn reserved for that occasion, and this is also the only time the family prays together. "We go around the table, offering prayers to everyone from the president to a favorite grandmother," says L'Tishia. After dinner, the family often goes on a special outing, like a walk to the park.

Social Justice Night

The Vogts of Covington, Kentucky, started weekly family nights to pass on Catholic religious traditions to their four kids. Family night starts by lighting a candle, then the family sings "Jesus Christ is the light of the world." Each week is devoted to a single topic, often related to peace or social justice, that is explored with a Bible verse and then a related activity. The theme might be an upcoming holiday, or the hurt of racism. One night the theme was blindness, and family members took turns being blindfolded (see box on page 105).

Family Home Evenings

Like many Mormons, the Hilton family of Las Vegas has these weekly family get-togethers on Monday. The children are young, so they last only about 20 minutes, including a special treat. The kids take turns picking a song and a prayer, while Nanette Hilton or her husband chooses the lesson. "It might be a lesson about honesty, or if a grandparent has died, the topic might be death," says Nanette.

Family Banner

Deborah Pecoraro is Catholic and started weekly family nights when the family lived in a predominantly Mormon area. "My kids felt prejudice from some of the Mormon kids, and we wanted to make them proud of their own religion," she says. Deborah took her theme from a Catholic prayer titled "God Made Us a Family," and created a special family banner out of felt. On family nights, dinner is served early and the kids get into their pajamas. They sing special songs and say a prayer. On some evenings, they look at family photographs or play games.

How to Make a Family Banner

One of the purposes of family night is to create a feeling of team spirit, a sense of shared beliefs, and your banner will help express that.

Materials

At a fabric or craft store, buy 2 yards (6 feet) of felt in the color you want for a background. Banners are long but skinny, so you will want to cut the fabric at home so that it's 5 or 6 feet long, by about 2 feet. Also buy scraps or small squares of other colors, including white and black.

Instructions

Design: Plan your design on paper first. Give each family member some space, perhaps 12 inches square, in which to create their self-portrait. Save space above, below, or between the portraits for the family name and logo. A logo might include symbols of your heritage, like a shamrock for Irish roots.

Cutting: Have everyone cut out the felt to make their portraits, including details like neckties, hats, and baseball bats. Add pets or favorite toys in felt. Glue them to the background.

Hanging: Cut three or four felt pieces 2 inches wide and 3 inches long. Fold them in half, then stitch or staple to the back of the banner, forming loops. Buy a dowel rod from the hardware store to slip through the loops and hang your banner—all the time or just for meetings.

Weekly Family Meetings

Family meetings may include similar elements like prayers and snacks, but tend to have "family business" as their central purpose. That includes dealing with issues like scheduling, finances, and behavior. This is a fabulous forum for airing your core values, and a great way to practice communication skills. Steven Covey, author of *The Seven Habits of Highly Effective Families*, says that regular family meetings help kids move from "me" to "we" in their thinking.

Ten Guidelines for Great Family Meetings

1. Everyone gets a say, but Mom and Dad have the last word.

2. Start by sharing the best thing that happened to you all week.

3. Meetings should be brief for young kids, maybe 15 minutes, but keep the pace brisk and businesslike generally.

4. Go over the week's outings, sports practices, doctor appointments, etc., with the family calendar on the table.

5. Take turns being the leader when the kids are old enough.

6. State problems without blaming, then brainstorm together. One child might say, "It's a problem that I'm the only one who washes the dishes." He should explain why this is a problem, and the family can jointly discuss solutions.

7. Give a "family star of the week" award for the most awesome accomplishment.

8. Take five minutes to discuss big-picture questions such as: Where should we go for summer vacation? Is it time to get a dog?

9. End with a fun activity and/or dessert treat. This could also be when allowance is paid out.

10. Keep next week's agenda on the refrigerator; anyone can add to it.

Tip: Barring emergencies, have the meeting at the same time and place every week! Better to have a mini-meeting than get in the habit of skipping.

More Ideas for Family Meetings

Say Something Nice

In the Brosbe family, you have to start the family meeting by saying something nice about someone else. Ellen Brosbe says, "It might be mundane stuff like 'thanks for letting me play your video game' but it's important for them to thank each other." The four kids have to take turns sharing a bedroom, so "rotating rooms" is almost always on the weekly agenda. Other issues that get discussed are everything from reminders to refill the orange juice pitcher to broad discussions like "Should we keep going to synagogue?" Ellen says her kids began getting surly about meetings when they reached their teens, but she says a lot of family issues got ironed out at these weekly sessions.

A Tradition of Debate

The Vogts had weekly family nights *plus* weekly meetings. Heidi Vogt, daughter of Susan, says that she and her three siblings got annoyed that family meetings were undemocratic. "We would bring up things we wanted, but they would vote us down even though we were the majority," says Heidi. "But we did get a chance to express our views, and I see now that it gave me a sense of what they really valued. We could never get them to put in cable TV, but they explained it's because they felt they had better uses for that money."

Susan Vogt gathered justice-themed family activities into a terrific book called *Just Family Nights*. It has more than 60 different ideas for family nights from her family and many others.

Dealing with Grumps

The Hassell family always starts their Monday family meetings with a prayer. The kids take turns being in charge of refreshments and supplying a good discussion topic, which includes major family purchases. If one of the children shows up at the meeting in a bad mood, "we have a family discussion about how to treat someone who is grumpy," says Mary Bliss Hassell, and they soon bring the defiant one into the fold.

An excellent resource is *Our Family Meeting Book: Fun and Easy Ways to Manage Time, Build Communication and Share Responsibility* by Elaine Hightower and Betsy Riley.

How to Make and Use a Talking Stick

One of the hardest tasks for young children is taking turns, and learning to listen to others when they urgently want to speak themselves. The talking stick is a traditional Native American sacred object that can be a magical tool in family meetings. Whoever is holding the stick and ONLY that person has the authority to speak. The stick is a visual reminder to focus on that person, who is supposed to speak truth from their heart. Children love the textures of the stick, and the feeling of literally holding power in their hands.

Materials

Get a thick stick, about an inch in diameter and 10 to 12 inches long (though traditional ones tend to be longer), from your backyard or local park. Smooth the ends with sandpaper, making sure there are no sharp edges or splinters. Get bright ribbons from a fabric or craft store, plus feathers from your yard or the store. Also use shells, beads, buttons, or other adornments.

Instructions

Wrap ribbons up the stick as far as you wish for smoothness and color, then let each family member choose one color of ribbon to represent their "voice," and tie that ribbon tightly to the stick. Spread these ribbons out, so each has its own space. Add as many feathers and other decorations as you want, to the ends or all over. Personalize the stick for your family, perhaps tying on a small stone from your yard, a few hairs from your dog, whatever suits you.

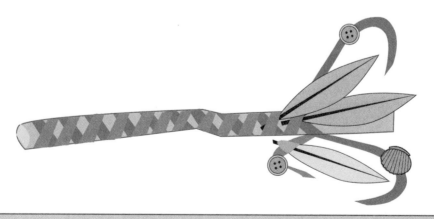

How to Use a Talking Stick

Traditionally, Native Americans sit in a circle when using a talking stick, and this works well. The circle is found over and over in the natural world, and each person in a circle has the same importance. You may wish to have a ritual way of starting the talking stick circle, as simple as holding hands for a moment or bowing to one another before you sit. You can sit on the floor, or at a table.

Decide on who will start, whether it's youngest or oldest, or take turns going first. You may hold the stick any way you choose, but the traditional way is to hold the stick vertically, as though it were planted in the earth. After the first person speaks, they look directly into the eyes of the next person before passing on the stick. Anyone who doesn't wish to speak may pass the stick along silently. One idea is to use the talking stick just at the beginning of your meeting, as you share your thoughts, feelings, and news with one another. Put the stick aside as you move on to issues of family business, games, a snack, and so forth.

Caution: Supervise young children carefully. Preschoolers may get carried away while talking and whack a neighbor accidentally. Younger children may do better with a soft "talking object." I would change the object rather than the practice of holding the thing without assistance.

Display: You may want to display your beautiful stick by hanging it from a nail or hook. Some families hang it only on Family Meeting days, as a visual reminder.

Want to learn more?

One family's account of how they use the stick is found at www.spiritseeker.com/feb-mar99/mary.htm. You can learn more about Native American traditions by going to www.yahooligans.com and finding their section on cultures and traditions.

Monthly Rituals

A month is a naturally powerful, logical unit of time, measured by the cycles of the moon. The good thing about a monthly ritual is that it's regular but there is lots of time for anticipation and preparation. For me, monthly rituals make sense for things that are extremely important but not my very highest priority.

Full Moon Bonfires

Small children are fascinated by the full moon and other celestial phenomena. The James family of Spokane, Washington, started having these bonfires when their son was six. The family of four makes a small fire right in the driveway on the night of a full moon, and toasts hot dogs and marshmallows on skewers.

First Day Wishes

Decorate a small shoebox or cigar box and keep it in the family room. Every month on the first day, have everybody in the family write on a piece of paper three goals they have for that month. It can be a task at school or work you hope to accomplish, improvement in a bad habit, but always something in the power of the individual to do; don't allow it to become a list of "things" your kids hope they receive as gifts. Each month as you fill out a new list, check how you did the previous month.

King or Queen for the Day

Each month, one of Cindy Whaling's kids gets to be royalty for a day. When a new month starts, the child whose turn it is grabs the calendar, closes his or her eyes, and points to a date. Cindy draws a tiny crown on that date, with the kid's name. The royal child gets to pick the dinner and activities they wish. As they get older, they wisely learn to point at weekends, when sleepovers are allowed, says Cindy. Her youngest always wants to go to McDonald's for a Happy Meal, which is considered too unhealthy on ordinary days.

Calendars for Kids

At an early age, kids want to know what's ahead and to follow along with the family's schedule. It's a great idea and a fun project to make a special calendar for each child to keep in their room.

You can do it one month at a time, using colored construction paper. As you make each month's sheet you can talk about what season that month is in, what holidays are coming, when family members have birthdays and anniversaries, and so forth.

Materials

Construction paper; ruler; crayons or markers; thin ribbon.

Instructions

Print the name of the month at the top and use the ruler to draw boxes for each day of the month. Write the numbers in each box, but save room for your child to add stickers or drawings to illustrate important events. Make a small hole at the right and left top edges of the paper, and poke ribbon through the holes, knotting the two ends of ribbon. Hang on a nail or hook somewhere low enough for your child to reach it. Start a ritual of checkmarking or crossing off each day, perhaps just before bed. (Give them a washable marker, so your wall isn't ruined.)

Sam's October

Sunday	Monday	Tuesday	Wednesday	Thursday	Friday	Saturday
1	2	3	4	5	6	7
8	9	10	11	12	13	14
15	16	17	18	19	20	21
22	23	24	25	26	27	28
29	30	31				

Full Moon Walks

Craig Patchin wanted a special ritual to bring him closer to his children, and spotted his chance when his oldest child was about to turn 10. His wife had bought a book called *Walk When the Moon Is Full* as a present for their daughter Bethany. Author Frances Hamerstrom, an ornithologist, wrote the book about the nature walks she took with her children during every full moon.

Inspired by this idea, Craig spontaneously wrote in the front of the book, "Happy Birthday. I make a pledge to you that we will go exploring every full moon this year. I love you, Daddy."

The Patchins live in a semirural area, and every month that year Craig and his daughter walked after dark, usually for at least half an hour. Often, they walked to the top of a hill in a nearby meadow where they could see for miles. Bethany loved the ritual so much that her younger sisters and brother could hardly wait for their turn, and they still remember many of the things they saw and heard and talked about.

Says Kelsey, Craig's third daughter, "One cold night when there was snow on the ground, we took a bunch of blankets and curled up in the hammock outside. My dad had to move a branch of the pine tree so we could see the moon, and we talked about memories and stories."

Now that all the Patchin kids have had their year of Full Moon Walks, they can't stand the idea of never doing it again. Plans are that the ritual will be repeated when they each turn 18.

Tip: Vary this ritual to suit yourselves. You can do this every month or just in nice weather. Take turns between the kids, month by month. You can take long or short walks, vary your path, perhaps stay close to home and use binoculars or a telescope to study the sky. Keep a journal about your Full Moon Walks.

More Monthly Rituals

Freedom Day

My son complained that he was overscheduled. "I go to school every day, karate on Saturday, and church on Sunday. When is it *my* day?" he wanted to know. So I designated the last Saturday of every month "Max Freedom Day" and he does what he wants (within reason). He usually skips karate, and I can't schedule hateful appointments like haircuts. The whining over scheduling is all but gone, and he has something to look forward to all month, every month.

Monthly Pizza Blast

We're all too busy to stay as close to our friends and neighbors as we'd like. One answer is no-fuss entertaining that is built into our schedules. Designate the first Friday or last Sunday of every month for your Family Pizza Party, but vary your guests. This is the time to meet a new neighbor, get to know the parents of your kids' best friends, invite the woman in your yoga class who looks interesting. Or ask the same four or five families, and rotate between each other's houses. Keep the menu simple: pizza, salad, and drinks.

Giving-Back Day

I heard about a family that does a monthly community service project. One day each month, the kids in the family fill "activity bags" with coloring books, crayons, and games, and deliver them to the local hospital for children who are patients. Other possibilities: Your kids can make monthly visits to a local nursing home and read to elderly residents. They could bake cookies monthly and deliver them to the local fire or police station. Or, sign up with a local environmental group to help clean up a nearby park. By going back to the same place, kids can form real relationships with those they help. (You may want to change the recipient of your help annually, as children grow and their interests change.)

Tip: For many more ideas, see *The Kid's Guide to Service Projects: Over 500 Service Ideas for Young People Who Want to Make a Difference.*

Family Book Groups

There is no more delightful or sustaining ritual in my life than my monthly reading group, and this is an idea that was made for families. Not only does it encourage the love of reading, but it provides a fun, regular activity for families. Unlike movies, there is a great deal of conversational give-and-take, and unlike such rituals as family meetings, parents get to interact more like friends than authority figures.

Mother-daughter book groups are popular now, especially with preteen girls. But father-son book groups are also a great idea. And you could form a book group that paired your entire family with several other families, providing the kids are close enough in age to enjoy the same books.

Six Simple Rules for Family Book Groups

1. The more authority kids have, the better. As much as possible, let them pick the books and lead the discussion.
2. Have members take turns being leader. The leader should prepare questions in advance to guide the discussion, and present some background about the author or book topic.
3. Serve a snack or meal before the discussion begins, and let the group members use this time for gossip and chitchat.
4. Once it's time to discuss the book, stick to the topic for at least half an hour. Be disciplined.
5. Don't get too big: if the group numbers more than 10, it will be hard to fit in your living room, and not everybody will get a say every month.
6. Respect everyone's opinion. No judging. Members can disagree without having an argument.

Tip: *The Mother-Daughter Book Club: How 10 Busy Mothers and Daughters Came Together to Talk, Laugh and Learn Through Their Love of Reading* has tons of good advice on forming a group and many book lists.

More on Family Book Groups

Five Good Questions to Ask About Any Book

1. Did you like the book? If so, why? If not, why not?

2. Which character was your favorite? Would you have behaved in the same way as that person?

3. Was there anything unusual in the way the author told the story? (flashbacks, multiple narrators, unusual slang, etc.).

4. How does this book compare to other books the group has read and discussed? Are the characters more or less believable? Which had the most exciting plot? Best ending?

5. What did you learn from this book? It could be something about an historical event, perhaps, or a sense of how other people live now and make choices in their lives.

Deciding What to Read

You can get a list of discussion-worthy books from your local library or bookstore. Many bookstores and libraries around the country also host intergenerational book groups on the premises.

There are lists of award-winning books at the American Library Association's website, at **www.ala.org/parents/**, but the best website I've found is **KidsReads.com**. This kid-friendly site reviews both new books and classics, provides extensive reading lists, and gives many tips on running a group.

Rites of Passage

The major recurring theme of human life is change, and rites of passage help us to celebrate and fully experience each major change as it happens. By staging meaningful rites of passage for our children starting at a young age, we teach them how to flexibly and creatively welcome change all their lives.

It has been said that modern societies have largely lost the ability to create deeply meaningful coming-of-age ceremonies. But I see many families and religious communities struggling to make workable contemporary rites of passage and succeeding. And I think families can produce enormously powerful rites of their own.

Childhood Milestones

Change is both scary and exciting. Our kids want to be "big," but they're frightened of that unknown place. Modest rituals can help them make the leap, and feel celebrated. If your child is having a rough time with one of these transitions, don't push or make them feel they've failed; celebrate that they're trying—and consult your pediatrician for advice.

Bye-bye Pacifiers

To get her daughter to give up her "sissies," Andrea Majewski told the girl that if she left the pacifiers in a special box for the Easter bunny, she'd get extra treats. The box was set out on Easter Eve, and next morning, sitting next to the Easter basket was the same box. The pacifiers were gone, but the box was full of special candy and a note from the Easter bunny about how grown-up the girl was. The girl was thrilled, and her little brother was eager to follow this magical ritual a few years later.

Big Boy Day/Big Girl Day

Experts say the best way to improve our kids' behavior is to "catch" them being good, and praise them immediately. If you're trying to help them grow out of a behavior like thumb-sucking or needing a pacifier, talk about how once they get through an entire day without doing this thing, they'll be celebrated as "Big Boy of the Day" after supper. The celebration could include a treat food, a special crown, or a privilege like extra story time. If there's a "big kid" activity they've been wanting to try such as a sport or helping you cook, pin that experience to a full week without the baby habit.

Bottles to Cups

Have the child help pick out a special "big girl" or "big boy" plastic cup, perhaps one illustrated with a favorite character. Tell him or her that new babies are being born in the world who really need their bottles. If there are no baby siblings, have them pretend to use a bottle to feed a doll or stuffed animal "baby." Pack up all the old bottles in a box and leave them by the front door at bedtime; help them invent a little good-bye song for the bottles. The next morning, serve the child's favorite drink in the new cup, with a fancy straw.

Coming-of-Age Rituals

First Period

The older our children get, the more vital it becomes that they help shape their role in any rituals they perform. That is especially true with coming-of-age rituals. After all, these rituals emerge from and celebrate a primal impulse to separate from one's parents. We defeat the purpose and power of such rites of passage if we deny our children a voice in how they ritually dramatize their coming independence.

Especially delicate is the question of creating ceremonies to celebrate a girl's first period. There are organizations around the country that stage group womanhood rituals involving girls and their parents. And this is fine, if the girl is comfortable.

But most of the teen girls I know are extremely shy about this private matter. However you honor this milestone, be sure to include some frank talk about the responsibilities that go along with this new stage in life, and the dangers.

Private Time

DeeAnn Pochedly let her daughter play hooky the day she got her first period, and took the girl out to lunch for a private celebration. As a gift, she gave her daughter pretty, colored underpants "to wear on those special days." DeeAnn says the event brought them closer: it was the first time in ages her daughter called her "Mommy."

Bejeweled

Marilyn Clark and her husband have accompanied each of their girls to a jewelry store to pick out a ring as soon as they start their period. Wearing the ring reminds the girls that their womanhood is worthy of celebration, but no one else needs to know the significance of the ring. I know another family where the girls get rubies, the red being symbolic of blood.

Tip: An especially good book to give girls waiting for the big change is *The Period Book: Everything You Don't Want to Ask But Need to Know*. It was co-written by an aunt and her 15-year-old niece.

Circle of Elders

In one Kentucky family, an all-women dinner is held when a girl is about to start menstruating. The older women share stories of their periods and offer advice. The girl is given gifts, and expected to phone all those women relatives when her period actually arrives.

A New Name

The Gardiner family of Stanchfield, Minnesota, takes this milestone very seriously and has created a detailed coming-of-age program. This might be awkward if there were any boys in the family, but with all girls, it's been lovingly embraced. Barbara Gardiner and her husband Kevin spend time with each girl before the period starts, reading and discussing a book called *What's Happening to My Body? for Girls*. As a family, they talk about how the change to womanhood is also a time of mental and emotional challenge and encourage the girls to try new sports and other activities. Also, each girl is allowed to choose a new middle name, based on a sense of her emerging adult personality. On the day the blood comes, there is a special family dinner, flowers are brought home by the father, and the girls get a special gift from Dad.

Flower Ceremony

There is a lovely first-period ritual for a mother and daughter in the book *I Am Woman by Rite: A Book of Woman's Rituals* by poet Nancy Brady Cunningham. On the same day the period starts, she suggests the girl and mother go to a quiet room after supper and light two red candles. Then the girl takes some red roses from a vase and cuts off the stems, symbolizing letting go of childhood. She lets the rose blossoms float in a glass bowl filled with water, "honoring her ability to bring forth life from her womb." Other elements suggested by Cunningham include giving the girl gifts of a new brush, comb, and mirror, and having the mother brush her hair. To suggest that womanhood will bring both sweet and bitter experiences, the mother feeds the girl a series of things from a spoon: bitter tea, salty water, and last, honey.

Coming-of-Age Rituals for Boys and Girls

In Japan, there is a national holiday every year to celebrate adulthood for those turning 20. America has nothing like it, though some religious and ethnic groups have deeply meaningful coming-of-age rites. These include the bar mitzvah and bat mitzvah for Jewish children, the vision quest still practiced by many Native Americans, and the Quinceañera, a lavish celebration for 15-year-old girls in the Latino community. The thoughtful rituals on the next several pages could be adapted for either sex.

Manhood Trip

The summer after they turned 13, the sons of John Fergus-Jean of Columbus, Ohio, were taken on a three-week camping trip out west alone with their dad. The destination each time was Yellowstone Park, but the route wasn't preplanned. Along the way, father and son read about Native American manhood rituals, and talked about how boys don't have a single milestone to signify maturity, as girls do. Each boy found a "secret spot" within Yellowstone and engaged in a physical challenge, jumping from the cliffs above Fire Hole River. They both smoked their first cigar with their father, and talked about the ritual history of tobacco, and the importance of handling its power in an adult way. John says the trips deepened his relationships with both sons.

Cutting Dad's Hair

Richard Boardman, a guidance counselor from Wisconsin, wanted a hands-on ritual that would signify the passing on of power to his children. When they complete eighth grade, they give him "the haircut of their choice." He literally puts his head in their hands. Naturally, the kids love it, threatening wild hairstyles for months in advance. The rules are that their father has to wear the resulting cut for a week without revisions, though he can wear a hat in public.

African-American Coming-of-Age

Charles Nabrit and Paula Penn-Nabrit of Columbus, Ohio, created an unusually rigorous and academic rite of passage. At 13, each of their three sons had to study scripture and African-American history, reading 16 assigned books and writing reports about them over six to nine months. Both a ceremony and a party capped each boy's efforts, and the ceremony included a speech given by the boy to family and friends. The Nabrit boys grumbled for years about how hard they had to work, but every one later attended a top Ivy League college.

Vision Quest: Adapting the Native American Tradition

When done creatively and with conviction, this ancient tradition can translate powerfully into modern life. The basic elements of vision quest are similar to that of many tribal coming-of-age rituals around the world.

The ritual includes a period of preparation and learning with the help of a mentor/elder, followed by a difficult physical trial designed to push the initiate past his normal limits. Often, Native American questers go alone into the wilderness to fast for days, seeking a vision of their future (and a new name). They return, share stories about their experience, and are welcomed and celebrated as an adult by their tribe.

In our culture, it's important that the teens be treated differently in some way after the ritual by their parents, perhaps given new privileges in the household.

One Mother's Version of Vision Quest

Before her oldest son turned 13, Diane Sanson of Malibu, California, decided she wanted to create a coming-of-age ritual for him and a group of his peers. The ritual took nine months to complete for five boys and their fathers. Once a month, the boys and men met in a "council," discussing everything from what it means to be a man in our society, to the series of challenges the boys would undertake. The challenges included camping and kayaking. Each boy had to perform some sort of community service, and each kept a journal about the process and their dreams and goals. Several times, the boys were taken to a cliff above the ocean at dawn, and given 45 minutes of quiet time to work on their journals. There was also a "sweat lodge" ceremony, performed by a hired Native American guide, in which the boys sat in a canvas "lodge" full of steamy heat. A big party was the final event, at which each boy spoke about what he had learned, and what sort of man he wanted to become.

Tip: Vision quest leaders are popping up everywhere. Check their credentials carefully. One resource is The School of Lost Borders in California, which has a 30-year track record. Go to **www.schooloflostborders.com** or call 530-305-4414.

A California father, Bernard Weiner, created a weekend manhood rite for a group of fathers and their teen boys (including his son). Among other things, they acted out different concepts of manhood. A slim book by Weiner called *Boy into Man* describes the rituals, and what the boys thought of them.

Vision Quest Resources

If your pre teen or teen is interested in exploring this possibility, you won't find a better guidebook than *The Thundering Years: Rituals and Sacred Wisdom for Teens* by Julie Tallard Johnson, a Wisconsin psychotherapist. It is packed with advice on meditation, writing a journal, and spiritual ways of exploring nature, but the section on rite-of-passage ceremonies is particularly strong. Excerpts from her book and other info can be found at **www.thunderingyears.com.**

Julie suggests that teens start planning their coming-of-age ritual months in advance, and that they choose a "wisdomkeeper" or mentor, "who represents the qualities of an adult that you aspire to." She says the most important aspect of the trial or challenge is that it be "bigger than anything you've done before . . . something that pushes you beyond your comfort level."

Here are some of the possible trials she suggests:

- sleeping under the stars alone
- running a race, a marathon, or a designated distance alone
- giving a performance of some kind
- doing your first hunt
- writing an article for the local paper
- mountain climbing, rafting, or kayaking (all which you've prepared for)
- creating some artistic piece (painting, sculpture, poetry, a play)

How to Make a Ribbons-of-Love Curtain

When someone we love reaches a significant milestone, we are sometimes at a loss as to how to celebrate. Just getting a fancier gift than usual seems insufficient. This is a ritual gift that also provides a ritual activity and is best done when you want the celebrated person to feel embraced by a whole community of family and friends. It would be a great activity to cap a coming-of-age ritual.

Materials

Extra-wide ribbon in bright colors (from a craft or sewing store) cut to lengths of 4 feet; glue; pens or markers; a wooden dowel rod half an inch to 1 inch in diameter and from 3 to 6 feet long, depending on how many people will participate.

Instructions

When you are finished, the dowel rod will be covered by a row of bright ribbons, hanging down like a beaded curtain. Unlike a maypole, where all the ribbons are attached to the top of a vertical pole, these ribbons will dangle down all along a horizontal pole. The ribbons will have writing on them: every family member and friend will take one ribbon and be given instructions on what to write, such as "something you wish for (the celebrated person) in the future" or "a quality you love about (the person)." For many milestone celebrations in our lives, there are friends and family who simply cannot come, so you'll want to send ribbons by mail ahead of time, for those who can't make it but want to express their love. (And you can always add some ribbons after the event, if they don't arrive till after the party.)

You may choose to attach the ribbons ahead of time and present the finished ribbon curtain to the honoree, or you could opt to make the finishing of the curtain part of your celebration. Perhaps each celebrant could come forward with their ribbon, reading out the sentiments written there. In any case, you will wrap the ribbon around the rod and attach it using craft or fabric glue; make sure the ribbon reaches over the top and covers part of the back of the wooden rod.

When completed, this ribbon curtain will be a gorgeous keepsake that can be hung in the child's room by two nails.

More Coming-of-Age Rituals for Girls

Sparklers in the Sand

The day my niece Jenny turned 13, her mother and I were sharing a condo on the beach in North Carolina, so I created a ceremony there. We asked Jenny to write down things and feelings from her childhood she was ready to leave behind, and she took these private papers and threw them in the ocean (I now regret this pollution, and wish we had burned them instead). After dark, I drew a circle in the sand, marking it with shells, candles, and sparklers, and we stood in the middle, facing each other. I brought a bottle of red (for blood) wine, and poured us each a little. As the sparklers burned, I toasted Jenny and spoke about the awesome woman I knew she would become. We sat on the beach for a long time afterward talking. Later, I gave Jenny 13 symbolic gifts, including a tiny globe because I hope she gets to travel a lot, a red rose for her beauty, etc.

Scarf Ceremony

This would work great for a group of girlfriends and family, as part of a celebration. Instruct each invitee to bring a beautiful scarf for the girl, something light in weight like chiffon or silk. Tie all the scarves together, making one long, colorful "rope."

As the girl stands still, have her hold one end of the scarf rope, while the girls and women wrap it around and around her, covering her. Tell her that as she moves forward through life, into independence, she will always be embraced by this community of loving women. Then, help her unwrap the scarves and run forward, trailing them like a banner.

Circle of Love

I love the smooth solidity of river rocks. If you don't live near a river, you can buy them by the pound from a plant nursery or landscaper. Buy enough for each person attending your ceremony, and let everybody paint one word with permanent paint. The word could be something you hope for that girl. Have the participants place the stones in a circle around the honored girl, one rock at a time. Standing in a bigger circle, the girls and women can give toasts or words of love. Later, the girl can display the rocks in a bowl or plant them in a garden.

Rituals for New Drivers

Car accidents are the leading cause of death for teenagers, but studies show that "parental involvement" can reduce the risks. Special rituals can help you celebrate the milestone of a first driver's license while preparing your kids for a huge new responsibility. In our culture of speed and mobility, earning a driver's license is a major rite of passage, and deserves to be recognized as such.

Prayer for a New Driver

In the Vogt family, a new driver is celebrated with a brief ceremony in which they are given not only a car key of their own, but a house key as well. The ceremony is part of a special dinner, with treat foods. Most of the family's rituals include a religious element, and this one is no exception. Susan Vogt's simple prayer goes: "God bless our child as he gains independence at this new stage in life, and bless this car, and keep our son safe in his travels."

Fitting Gifts

Whether you celebrate with a little family party or dinner out, there are a number of things that would make meaningful gifts for a new driver, such as a special key ring. In addition, you might get a fancy set of tools and safety gear, things like flares.

A New Driver's Contract

However you celebrate, one vital aspect of the ceremony is the solemn signing of a pact between the parents and the new driver. The elements should be discussed and understood in advance, but you may want to read it aloud and have the new driver verbally agree to each statement, like taking a vow. The glove compartment might be a good place to keep the contract, as a reminder.

Usually, such contracts include an agreement to observe all motor vehicle laws. Sometimes they spell out the consequences of breaking such laws. In the Chesto family, each kid was allowed one speeding ticket and one fender-bender, but anything beyond that resulted in reduced driving privileges.

Other ideas for the contract: regulation of how many passengers are allowed, how far the teenager is allowed to drive, and rules for driving after dark.

Here is a contract written by one of Kathy Chesto's daughters, when she was a teenager. It could easily be modified:

I believe that driving a car is a serious responsibility, to myself, to passengers in the car, to those in other vehicles, to pedestrians, and to the environment.

I believe that traffic laws have been made for our protection, and I will obey them.

I believe that others have as much right to the road as I do and I will attempt to always be courteous.

I believe that a car is a means of transportation, not a symbol of power, and I will use it wisely and share in the responsibility of being a driver in this family.

I believe that a car is an expense that should be shared justly by all who use it.

I believe that the less parents know, the more they worry, and I will try my best to call when I am late and keep them informed.

Graduations

All graduations are rites of passage. And though I remember laughing at lavish graduation ceremonies for five-year-olds, I did give a pizza party when my son finished nursery school. For each child, I made a "medal," which consisted of a gold construction-paper star, to which I glued a blue ribbon. "Crossroads Graduate" was written in the star's center, and each child had one of these draped around his or her neck. In addition to the pizza, someone brought a giant chocolate chip cookie with "Congratulations" written in frosting.

A high school graduation is another thing entirely. Indeed, it's one of the only ceremonial occasions (outside of weddings) for which we still dress up. Wearing caps and gowns as they walk alone past a roomful of classmates and family, teenagers find themselves physically enacting the crossing of a major threshold toward independence and adulthood. For many, it's a powerful emotional experience.

But I think families can do a lot to enhance that experience, helping their graduates to celebrate their past and eagerly anticipate the future—to acknowledge in some ceremonial way that though a separation is coming, the love and devotion of the family will follow them wherever life's journey takes them.

Graduation Letters

Three months before her daughter graduated from high school, Betty Ruddy sent a note to the girl's relatives and close family friends asking them to write a letter in honor of her graduation. Some wrote the girl advice for the future, and others shared favorite memories of her childhood. One aunt sent a poem, while another made up a mock "report card" charting the girl's triumphs and character traits. Betty gathered all these papers into a beautiful box, and presented it to the girl as one of her graduation gifts. "She was in tears before she unfolded the third letter," Betty writes in a column about "Rituals for Celebrating Teens" at **www.parentingteens.com**.

124

Bonfire of Childhood

As part of a party involving a group of close friends, you might build a fire (in a safe place) and have all the graduates write on slips of paper aspects of their childhoods they are ready to let go.

Knowledge Threshold

Think of a special threshold you can create that is symbolic of where your teenager is headed next. If your son is headed off to mechanic's school, maybe get big sheets of cardboard and paint car logos or a car engine on the front. Tape the cardboard over the entrance to a door, leaving a gap for the graduate to "cross the threshold " to their future. If your child is heading to college, create a threshold using sheets or cardboard that is a listing of great works of literature or other subjects they're likely to seek out.

Gifts of Values

One of the greatest gifts we give our children over the years is the values we teach and share. Find a way to symbolically present your graduating teen with a reminder of the gifts of character they carry inside, such as giving them a slim, blank book in which you write one value on each page. When Kathleen Chesto's children went off to college, she gave each one a basket of essentials for dorm life, things like shampoo and a dustpan. As she gave them the gifts, she voiced a parental wish with each one: "I give you this soap. Never be afraid to get your hands dirty in the service of others."

Great Graduation Gifts to Start in Kindergarten

Novelist Jean Hanff Korelitz writes a letter every year to her children on their birthdays and keeps them sealed and hidden away. Another mother I know asked each of her children's teachers to write a letter about her child at year's end, and she saves all those letters from kindergarten on. High school graduation is a logical time to gather together such material that documents a complete childhood, along with a collage of school photos from every year, and present them to your amazed child.

Acknowledgments

My help on this book came from many sources, but particularly from a group of brilliant and inventive mothers I got to know while reporting on rituals for magazine articles and my first book. They have stayed in touch with me and continue to share their thoughtful rituals by e-mail and phone and, when I'm lucky, in person.

I'm especially grateful to Lucy Steinitz, Elinor Craig, L'Tishia Suk, Barb Brock, Monica Hall, Gail Simpson, Susan Vogt, and Kathleen Chesto. I wish I could invite you all to a party and create a gratitude ritual. I'm also inspired by the many subscribers to my e-mail newsletter who share their traditions month after month.

This book would not exist without the energy and commitment of my editor, Lynn Rosen, who was determined to make it happen. I thank you from the bottom of my heart. Also instrumental was Geri Thoma, my agent and friend, who shares the delicious monthly ritual of our reading group.

Big thanks to the group of family and friends who make up my indispensable support system. They include my incredible sister Tracy Hagen-Smith, my stepdaughter Kate Leone, and her mother, Anita Leone. Thanks also to my dear, devoted friends Jean Hanff Korelitz, Wendy Kwitny, Naomi Drew, Dick Einhorn, Ann Hagedorn, Jill Ciment, Carol Mason, Joan Kron, and Laura Szabo-Cohen. You keep me going.

Finally, my deepest love and thanks go to my husband, Richard Leone, and my son, Max. You make life worth living and ritual worth creating.

How to Reach the Author/Subscribe to Free Newsletter

You can write to Meg Cox via e-mail at **megmaxc@aol.com**, or in a letter, to her publisher, Running Press, 125 South 22nd Street, Philadelphia, PA 19103. She is always interested in hearing about thoughtful and inventive family traditions. If you wish to subscribe to the free monthly e-mail newsletter, Meg Cox's Ritual Newsletter, please write to Meg at the above e-mail address.

Selected Bibliography

Banks, Lynne Reid. *The Indian in the Cupboard*. New York, NY: Doubleday, 1985.

Braham, Clare Bonfanti, and Maria Bonfanti Esche. *Kids Celebrate!: Activities for Special Days Throughout the Year*. Chicago, IL: Chicago Review Press, 1998.

Bunting, Eve. *Night Tree*. San Diego, CA: Harcourt Brace and Co., 1991.

Bunting, Eve. *December*. San Diego, CA: Harcourt Brace and Co., 2000.

Chesto, Kathleen O'Connell. *Family Prayer for Family Times: Traditions, Celebrations and Rituals*. Mystic, CT: Twenty-third Publications, 1995.

Christopher, Doris. *Come to the Table: A Celebration of Family Life*. New York, NY: Warner Books, 1999.

Crichton, Jennifer. *Family Reunion: Everything You Need to Know to Plan Unforgettable Get-Togethers*. New York, NY: Workman Publishing, 1998.

Cunningham, Nancy Brady. *I Am Woman by Rite: A Book of Women's Rituals*. York Beach, ME: Red Wheel/Weiser, 1995.

Cuthbert, Susan, ed. *The Classic Treasury of Children's Prayers*. Minneapolis, MN: Augsburg Fortress Publishers, 2000.

Dodson, Shireen, with Teresa Barker. *The Mother-Daughter Book Club: How 10 Busy Mothers and Daughters Came Together to Talk, Laugh and Learn Through Their Love of Reading*. San Francisco, CA: HarperCollins Publishers, 1997.

Donahue, Shari Faden. *My Favorite Haggadah: A Fun Interactive Passover for Children and Their Families*. Washington Crossing, PA: Arimax Inc., 1995.

Drew, Naomi. *Hope and Healing: Peaceful Parenting in an Uncertain World*. New York, NY: Citadel Press, 2002.

Galinsky, Ellen. *Ask the Children: The Breakthrough Study That Reveals How to Succeed at Work and Parenting*. New York, NY: William Morrow & Co., 1999.

Gravelle, Karen, and Jennifer Gravelle. *The Period Book: Everything You Don't Want to Ask But Need to Know*. New York, NY: Walker & Co., 1996.

Haab, Sherri, and the Editors of Klutz. *Arts and Crafts Recipes (Klutz Guides)*. Palo Alto, CA: Klutz, Inc., 1998.

Hamerstrom, Frances. *Walk When the Moon Is Full*. Freedom, CA: Crossing Press, 1985.

Hightower, Elaine, and Betsy Riley. *Our Family Meeting Book: Fun and Easy Ways to Manage Time, Build Communication and Share Responsibility*. Minneapolis, MN: Free Spirit Publishing, 2002.

Ilnisky, Esther. *Let the Children Pray: How God's Young Intercessors Are Changing the World*. Ventura, CA: Regal Books, 2000.

Johnson, Julie Tallard. *The Thundering Years: Rituals and Sacred Wisdom for Teens*. Rochester, VT: Bindu Books, 2001.

Kohn, Alfie. *Punished by Rewards: The Trouble with Gold*

Stars, Incentive Plans, A's, Praise and Other Bribes. Boston, MA: Houghton Mifflin, 1993.

Lang, Virginia, and Louise Nayer. *How to Bury a Goldfish . . . and 113 Other Family Rituals for Everyday Life*. Emmaus, PA: Daybreak, a division of Rodale Books, 2000.

Lewis, Barbara A. *The Kid's Guide to Service Projects: Over 500 Service Ideas for Young People Who Want to Make a Difference*. Minneapolis, MN: Free Spirit Publishing, 1995.

Milne, A.A. *The Complete Tales of Winnie-the-Pooh*. New York, NY: Penguin, 1996.

Milne, A.A. *The Complete Poems of Winnie-the-Pooh*. New York, NY: Dutton Books, 1998.

Morgan, George E. *Your Family Reunion: How to Plan It, Organize It, and Enjoy It*. Orem, UT: Ancestry Publishing, 2001.

Nelson, Gertrud Mueller. *To Dance with God: Family Ritual and Community Celebration*. Mahwah, NJ: Paulist Press, 1986.

Ryan, M.J., ed. *A Grateful Heart: Daily Blessings for the Evening Meal from Buddha to the Beatles*. Berkeley, CA: Conari Press, 1994.

Seibold, J. Otto, and Vivian Walsh. *Olive, the Other Reindeer*. San Francisco, CA: Chronicle Books, 1997.

Shaw, Nancy. *Sheep in a Jeep*. Boston, MA: Houghton Mifflin, 1986.

Singleton, Suzanne. *Clever Party Planning: Ideas and Themes for Kids, Teens and Adults*. Glencoe, MD: TwentyNine Angels Publishing, 1999.

Strassfield, Michael. *The Jewish Holidays: A Guide and Commentary*. San Francisco, CA: HarperCollins Publishers, 1985.

Trelease, Jim. *The Read-Aloud Handbook*. New York, NY: Penguin Books, 1982.

Van Allsburg, Chris. *The Polar Express*. Boston, MA: Houghton Mifflin, 1985.

Vogt, Susan. *Just Family Nights*. Elgin, IL: Brethren Press, 1994.

Wall, Kathleen, and Gary Ferguson. *Lights of Passage: Rituals and Rites of Passage for the Problems and Pleasures of Modern Life*. San Francisco, CA: HarperCollins Publishers, 1994.

Warner, Penny. *The Kids' Pick-a-Party Book: 50 Fun Party Themes for Kids, Ages 2 to 16*. Minnetonka, MN: Meadowbrook Press, 1998.

Weiner, Bernard. *Boy into Man: A Father's Guide to Initiation of Teenage Sons*. Penryn, CA: Personal Transformation Press, 1992.

White, E.B. *Trumpet of the Swan*. New York, NY: Harper Trophy, 2000.

Wiesel, Elie. *A Passover Haggadah*. New York, NY: Simon & Schuster, 1993.

Wojciechowski, Susan. *The Christmas Miracle of Jonathan Toomey*. Nashville, TN: Thomas Nelson, 1998.